CRAFT MOVES

Lesson Sets for Teaching Writing with Mentor Texts

Stenhouse Publishers
Portland, Maine

Stacey Shubitz

Foreword by
Lester Laminack

D1089369

Stenhouse Publishers
www.stenhouse.com

Library of Congress Cataloging-in-Publication Data
Names: Shubitz, Stacey, 1977– author.
Title: Craft moves : lesson sets for teaching writing with mentor texts / Stacey Shubitz.
Description: Portland, Me. : Stenhouse Publishers, 2016. | Includes bibliographical references and index.
Identifiers: LCCN 2015048630 | ISBN 9781625310224 (pbk. : alk. paper)
Subjects: LCSH: Language arts (Elementary) | Composition (Language arts)—Study and teaching (Elementary) | Children's literature—Study and teaching (Elementary) | English language—Composition and exercises—Study and teaching (Elementary) | Picture books.
Classification: LCC LB1576 .S4145 2016 | DDC 372.62/3—dc23 LC record available at http://lccn.loc.gov/2015048630

Cover design, interior design, and typesetting by Martha Drury
Cover photograph by Daniel Shanken; author photograph by Ashley Gillman of Ashley Elizabeth Photography

Manufactured in the United States of America

 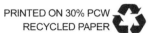

*For Marc Schaefer, who fills my life with love
and is always ready for a good story. I could not ask
for more.*

Contents

Foreword

Stacey Shubitz is a passionate learner. The need for insight and to understand inform her teaching, whether she is conferring with fifth-grade writers, coaching writing teachers, or leading a graduate class. It is no surprise to see her take ideas planted during a 2008 summer writing institute at Teachers College, nurture them with further professional reading, and cultivate them into rich and mature classroom practice.

Stacey is a thinker, a reflective practitioner who works with ideas and refines practice until it blossoms. As one member of the team behind the popular blog *Two Writing Teachers*, she is a consummate professional who shares her insights, new thinking, wonderings, and questions with other educators. Her writing voice is clear, unembellished, and offers practical classroom talk that makes her posts both appreciated and immediately practical.

You'll find that same voice here. In *Craft Moves*, Stacey talks to you as if you are sitting with her in a coffee shop after school. She'll chat a bit and give you just enough of the backstory to let you know who she is and how she has come to embrace this thinking and engage in these practices. She honors the voices who have helped her refine her own teaching, and then she leads you through her new thinking. She will stretch your understandings a bit and offer her signature practical suggestions that have the potential to lift both your teaching and your students' writing.

If you are reading this, it is safe to assume that you are familiar with mentor texts, craft moves, and the notion of reading like a writer. You've likely read books like *Wondrous Words* by Katie Wood Ray (1998), *Craft Lessons* by Ralph Fletcher and JoAnn Portalupi (1998, 2007), *Nonfiction Craft Lessons* by JoAnn Portalupi and Ralph Fletcher

(2001), *Mentor Texts* by Lynne Dorfman and Rose Cappelli (2007), *The Writing Thief* by Ruth Culham (2014), and my own *Cracking Open the Author's Craft* (2007). If you are reading this, it is safe to assume that you understand how picture books, poems, essays, information books, all-about books, novels, newspapers, op-ed articles, and basically anything in print can be studied closely—using a lens for "How and why did they do that?"—to extend your repertoire of craft moves.

So you may be asking yourself, *Why would I need to read another book on mentor texts and craft moves?* Here's why. Through her study of professional literature, her continued practice in the field, her work with teachers, and her own graduate studies, Stacey has pushed her thinking and deepened her understanding of what it means to work with mentor texts in our classrooms. She has delved into the idea that one book holds great potential for deep work. Stacey notes that Lucy Calkins planted this idea in her thinking during a summer institute at Teachers College in 2008. As a result, Stacey made it her mission to know a small collection of books intimately. She worked to discover how she and her students could return to the same book again and again for various purposes in mini-lessons, conferring, and small-group work. Though she cautions us to avoid "over-studying" a book to the point that we "extract the joy from reading like a writer," she demonstrates how a single book can become a treasured resource for many insights.

Working with a small set of books and coming to know them deeply leads to understandings that help you look at every other text with a new lens. Stacey began to notice that certain craft moves held more power to lift her students' writing. Being the passionate learner she is, Stacey delved into a study of picture books with attention to what she has come to call *power* craft moves. She offers no apologies for a devoted focus on picture books: "I believe picture books should be used as writing mentors in the upper elementary grades just as much as they're used in the primary grades, because many include sophisticated language, structures, and plot lines while providing the visual supports some upper elementary school students still need." Through this focused work, Stacey says, "I've come up with ten *power* craft moves for fiction and ten for nonfiction books, based on the things I hope to see in my students' writing, to help me determine what I can teach young writers from picture books . . . craft moves we want all young writers to have in their writer's toolbox."

As she leads us through the idea of using mentor texts to help young writers explore and own these craft moves, she points out that any book she uses as a mentor text must have at least six of the ten power craft moves in it. Those books that stand up to Stacey's criteria are integrated into the classroom through read-aloud and are available to students. Students come to think of the authors of these mentor texts as their writing colleagues. Stacey notes, "Their books inspire us, their personal stories and struggles resonate with us, and they show us new ways of understanding. We welcome authors we trust into our classrooms to help us teach our students new strategies to help them become better writers." If you are less familiar with picture books or don't yet feel confident about selecting mentor texts, Stacey offers a set of questions to consider as you launch your search for mentors in your classroom.

Stacey offers sage advice and supports her suggestions and assertions with professional literature. If you are less skilled with managing a writing workshop, you will find her sitting beside you, listening and speaking to your concerns. She offers multiple suggestions for organization, developing structures and routines, and managing small-group work and conferring, but the heartbeat of this work is found in her thinking about power craft moves. Chapters 5 and 6, which make up the majority of the text, are devoted to lifting out and making visible the insights Stacey has gleaned about the potential that can be found in a single well-chosen, deeply studied book. When you reach the final page of Stacey's book, your mind will be bubbling with new insights and you will be itching to go to your bookshelf and sit for hours with a small stack of your most well-loved picture books.

Lester Laminack
February 2016

Acknowledgments

I've come to believe that writing a book is a lot like being pregnant. It takes a long time to get from conception to delivery. In the grand scheme of things, it takes a short amount of time to birth a baby or a book. What makes both of these things—pregnancy and a publishing journey—possible are the relationships you have with other people.

Mary Napoli, my mentor from Penn State Harrisburg, encouraged me to write about the work and teaching I was doing surrounding mentor texts. She suggested I write a journal article. I went overboard and wrote a book instead! I appreciate your friendship, support, and encouragement, Mary.

A tremendous thank-you to Bill Varner, my editor, who worked with me for months to shape this book into what you hold in your hands. I am grateful for your guidance, your patience, and your vision. Also, a special thank-you to Holly Holland, who helped me revise this book with a fresh set of eyes.

Thanks to Nate Butler, Jacqueline Carr, Chris Downey, Louisa Irele, Jay Kilburn, Chuck Lerch, Chandra Lowe, Zsofi McMullin, Philippa Stratton, and Dan Tobin for the roles each of you has played from proposal through publication of this book. I am thankful to be part of the Stenhouse family.

My interest in mentor texts began when I was a fifth-grade teacher at P.S. 171 in Manhattan. My principal, Dimitres Pantelidis, supported me as I carried out a year-long action research project on using mentor texts to lift the level of my students' writing. I am grateful he allowed me to take risks as a teacher so I could improve my practice as well as my students' writing.

The ideas in this book are built on the remarkable work of Lucy Calkins, Rose Cappelli, Lynne Dorfman, Ralph Fletcher, and Katie Wood Ray. Their books—*The Art of Teaching Writing; Mentor Texts; Nonfiction Mentor Texts; Mentor Author, Mentor Texts;* and *Wondrous Words,* respectively—have been major influences on my thinking. An additional thank-you to Lynne and Rose, who have been both mentors and friends to me since I moved to Pennsylvania in 2009.

Though I know many of them will never see this, thank you to the authors and illustrators whose books inspired me. I have a tremendous respect for your work. Thank you for creating the twenty treasures for which I have written lessons. Many thanks to Niki Alicea for linking me up with some great educators. I appreciate Rhoda Barasch, Debbie Hervitz, Vicki Millard, Michael O'Brien, Nancy Snyder, and Rachel Zilbering for opening the doors of their schools to me. A special thanks to Angie Harrison, Brandy Hurley, Meg Rusanowsky, and Kelly Sherbo, whose students' work appears in this book.

It took almost three years from the day I proposed this book until the day I sent my manuscript in. (Thank goodness pregnancies don't last that long!) There were several highs and lows, unrelated to my writing life, during that time. A few people made it possible for me to keep pushing through. I thank Stacey Nolish Blank, Andrea Lieber, Lauren Lutz, Rachel Mandelman, Kathy Mathias, Lori Shienvold, Scott Shubitz (my little cousin who has become a friend), and Emily Kretchmer Winthrop for their understanding and encouragement.

Grace Enriquez was my very first instructor at Columbia University's Teachers College in 2005. Since that time, she's served as a mentor, expert recommender of picture books, and friend. Many thanks for all you've done for me through the years, Grace.

A sincere thank-you to the Slice of Life Community, which comes together on Tuesdays and for the entire month of March over at Two Writing Teachers. Your comments have fueled and encouraged me as a writer. I am grateful for each of you.

My Sunday night writing critique group—Julie Burchstead, Catherine Flynn, Melanie Meehan, and Margaret Simon—deserves my gratitude. Thank you, ladies, for keeping me going with my "other writing" while I was working on this book.

Anna Gratz Cockerille, Betsy Hubbard, Beth Moore, Dana Murphy, and Tara Smith came into my professional writing life through Two Writing Teachers in 2013. And then Deb Frazier and

Kathleen Sokolowski walked into it in 2015. Thank you for being brilliant educators and collaborators. I am fortunate to work with and learn from you.

My mother-in-law, Linda Schaefer, may have retired from being a literacy coach, but she still remains one of my go-to people when I have a question about the teaching of reading or writing. I appreciate your insight as an educator as well as your love and support.

Marcia and Gerald Shubitz, my parents, placed an importance on education for as long as I can remember. It is because of their influence that I am committed to being a lifelong learner. Thank you, Mom and Dad, for giving me life, guiding me, and helping me to realize my dreams.

My daughter, Isabelle, played a small but important role in this book. I thank her for listening to me read aloud many picture books—some of which she didn't want to hear at first—to gauge whether I could fall in love with a text enough to feature it in this book. Some of her favorites, like *Clever Jack Takes the Cake, Knuffle Bunny Free*, and *Stella Brings the Family*, appear in this book and were read many nights at bedtime, which helped me get to know them intimately.

My husband, Marc Schaefer, took Isabelle out to Sunday morning breakfasts at the local diner, did the weekend grocery shopping, and took her to more playgrounds and trampoline parks than I can count so I could have a quiet work space on Sunday mornings. This book would never have made it to Stenhouse on time without his help co-parenting our daughter. Marc was also the person who nudged me to take breaks and to step away from the computer whenever I spent too many hours in front of it. Thank you, Marc, for helping me achieve balance while writing this book. I celebrate the incredible spouse and friend you are.

Introduction

My first literacy coach, Pat Werner, placed books by some of the greats in my hands when I was a new classroom teacher. I'm fortunate she introduced me to the writings of Eve Bunting, Donald Crews, Angela Johnson, Patricia Polacco, and Cynthia Rylant during my first year. I quickly became obsessed with mentor texts, referring to the authors by their first names when I used their writing as examples during my mini-lessons and conferences.

I disseminated literacy interviews to my soon-to-be fifth graders in June 2006. I asked them what they had learned about writing from reading. One of my questions was:

> *Have you learned anything about writing from the books someone has read to you or you have read yourself? What have you learned? What is the best book you know that shows kids something about good writing?*

All (That's right, all thirty-two!) of my students claimed they had learned nothing about being a better writer from reading books. I was stunned because they had a reputation for being voracious readers. Once I calmed down, I became determined to help these students read like writers.

In fall 2006, I began my second year of studies in the literacy specialist program at Columbia University's Teachers College, which meant I had to start a Master's Action Research Project. I chose to embark on a yearlong journey to determine how mentor texts (published writing, my own writing, and other students' writing) could lift the level of my students' writing. I began reading picture books to my fifth graders, who were initially unenthusiastic since they insisted picture books were for babies. By the middle of the school year, however, my class of voracious readers had come around. They recognized the rich language and beauty that picture books offer. They began to ask "Can I borrow _____ because I like the way . . ." or to say things like "I'd like to use _____ as a mentor text because I like the way the writer writes." In June, my fifth graders completed their year-end writing self-evaluations. Many said they had learned more about writing by studying mentor texts, specifically picture books. I celebrated because I had invested a lot of sweat equity in my effort to transform their views about picture books.

I continued to collect picture books—new releases and older titles colleagues recommended—so I could serve as a purveyor of them for my students. But something else changed the way I thought about reading-writing connections. When I studied with Lucy Calkins at the 2008 Summer Institute for the Teaching of Writing, she said, "If you want to be clear, use more words." Calkins was referring to the way we talk with kids about mentor texts. She believed it was important to refrain from using jargon (e.g., "show, don't tell") when teaching kids how to make reading-writing connections. If children are going to internalize what we're teaching them, Calkins asserted, then we have to use more words—meaningful words—when we teach them how to carry out a craft move. Saying more helps students to develop true understanding.

That summer, I also learned that you could use one book for many purposes. No longer would I need to have a slew of mentor texts for every unit of study. Instead, Calkins helped me realize I could know a few books well and use those to teach a variety of craft moves to young writers in the following ways:

1. By talking about my interaction with a particular part of the text in a step-by-step way.
2. By pointing out what kinds of writerly choices the author made and why I think the author chose to write/craft in a particular way.
3. By naming the move the writer made in a way that will help students understand this craft move as it applies beyond the piece of writing we're looking at together (i.e., teach the writer, not the writing) in a whole sentence, not just with a term or some buzzwords (e.g., the "show, don't tell" power craft move) (Shubitz 2008)

This approach changed the way I used mentor texts with my students. I became more explicit in my explanations, which helped my students to understand what I wanted them to do as writers, not just on the text they were writing that day, but also on future texts they would compose.

A few years later, I taught a graduate course at Penn State Harrisburg titled Children's Literature in Teaching Writing. The capstone project for the course, which each student had to complete, was a set of lessons for an exemplary picture book that could serve as a mentor text in writing workshop. Each of my graduate students selected a picture book they admired and mined it for multiple craft moves they could teach young writers in one-to-one writing conferences or small-group lessons. The purpose of this assignment was twofold: First, my graduate students left the course with a teaching tool they could use with their students. Second, and more important, I wanted them to see how knowing one text really well could allow them to teach many lessons to their young writers.

I shared some of my grad students' lesson sets with my mentor Mary Napoli, who encouraged me to share my thinking about using one book to teach multiple things with a wider audience. Napoli realized the power of having just a few mentor texts with multiple teaching possibilities that teachers knew really well. With her encouragement, I started writing this book.

Don't Teach Writing Alone

Mentor texts are samples of exemplary writing we can study during writing workshops. Teachers use mentor texts to teach students how to lift the level of their writing. "Mentor texts help writers notice things about an author's work that is not like anything they might have done before, and empower them to try something new" (Dorfman and Cappelli 2007, 3). Mentor texts can be books, short stories, articles, letters, and so on. Basically any text that can teach students *how* to write well can serve as a mentor text.

I initially learned how to teach students to read like a writer from Katie Wood Ray. In *Wondrous Words* (1999), Ray says there are five parts to reading like a writer:

1. *Notice* something about the craft of the text.
2. *Talk* about it and *make a theory* about why a writer might use this craft.

3. Give the craft a *name*.
4. Think of *other texts* you know. Have you seen this craft before?
5. Try and *envision* using this craft in your own writing. (120)

Some teachers encourage students to dissect mentor texts in an effort to glean as much as possible from the writing. Yet over-studying a text can extract the joy from reading like a writer. Ralph Fletcher (2011) encourages kids to unpack texts, which means reading once for pleasure and at least once for craft. After talking about the craft with their teacher and their peers, students can interact with the text by annotating it, marking surprising things, circling words or phrases they like, or underlining sentences they admire. From there, Fletcher encourages students to:

• Make a copy of the writing and put it in your writer's notebook.
• Copy a sentence or short section of the piece in your writer's notebook, maybe mentioning why you chose it.
• Share it with a friend, zooming in on one part or craft element you really liked.
• "Write off the text"—that is, create a similar piece of your own. (13)

Allow your students to be inspired by texts prior to using them in small-group lessons. This will help increase their engagement and willingness to try out a specific craft move that you think will benefit them as writers.

Katie Wood Ray advises teachers to select mentor texts to help their students reach higher as writers. She states:

> *The bottom line for why I select the text is that I see something in* how that text is written *which would be useful to my students to also see. I see something about the text that holds potential for my students' learning. I am looking for texts that have something in them or about them that can add to my students' knowledge base of how to write well.* (1999, 188)

Student writing will only be as good as the mentor texts we share with our students. It's paramount to choose texts that will meet students where they're standing and guide them to grow as writers.

About the Twenty Books I've Selected

Picture books, by their very nature, are short. Most contain thirty-two pages worth of outstanding writing, which makes them ripe for classroom use. I used picture books with my fourth- and fifth-grade students. Although some of them initially thought picture books were immature, they grew to recognize the richness of the writing and embraced them as mentor texts. I believe picture books should be used as writing mentors in the upper elementary grades just as much as they're used in the primary grades, because many include sophisticated language, structures, and plotlines while also providing the visual supports some upper elementary school students still need.

All students deserve to read mirror books, in which they see themselves, and window books, in which they learn about others (Bishop 1990). This means teachers must have books that represent a variety of religions, races, and sexual orientations in mentor-text baskets during all months of the year, not just in those with special designations such as Black History Month or Women's History Month.

I spent much of 2014 and 2015 reading hundreds of picture books and selected those I thought would help students to learn craft moves that they could add to their writing repertoire. All the books I selected have been published since 2010. I've included books written by well-known, award-winning authors, as well as books written by emerging authors.

We Need Mentors

In "Using Authors as Mentors," Aimee Buckner writes:

> *In the fall, as my students and I get to know each other as readers and writers, I share with them the things I do as a reader and a writer. For example, I tell them about my mentors. I have mentors for teaching, mentors for parenting, and mentors for writing. We discuss what a mentor is and how mentors can help them become better readers and writers.* (1999, 7)

Everyone—adults and kids alike—needs to have at least one writing mentor. These may be people we know personally or authors we've never met but whose writing we know intimately. Either one is okay.

Our students don't stay with us forever. Helping students to use mentor texts well is one of the greatest gifts we can give them. First, we expose kids to lots of good writing when they're with us so they "develop an ear for what good writing sounds like" (Heard 2014, 8). Next, we show students how to make meaningful reading-writing connections as opposed to superficial ones (Calkins 1994). Finally, we teach them how to find their own mentor texts because they won't always have teachers to provide them as they move through their school careers and work lives. I believe young writers who learn to seek, use, and appreciate their own mentor texts will grow into adults who can notice what other writers do and then use that knowledge to enrich their own writing.

What's Next?

Chapter 1 suggests techniques that will help you craft your own small-group lessons so you can teach from picture books that you may encounter in the future. In addition, it also suggests techniques for finding favorite mentor texts and authors. Chapter 2 provides a discussion of picture books as a teaching tool and offers ways to integrate them into the curriculum, workshops, and classroom discussions. Chapter 3 provides information on routines and procedures you'll want to have in place so your students can focus their writing during the independent writing portion of writing workshop. Chapter 4 helps you prepare for small-group instruction. Chapters 5 and 6 contain 184 strategy lessons—from twenty different picture books—you can teach students to help them become better writers.

Are you ready to build a classroom culture where students learn to grow as writers using the skills of published authors? I anticipate the authors whose picture books are featured in this book will become like rock stars in your students' eyes. Be prepared to let authors inspire and energize your classroom. The power craft moves you teach your students will live in their writing toolboxes across this school year and for the rest of their lives.

Chapter 1

Choosing Picture Books for Mentor Texts

A few months ago I led a staff development seminar and talked about the importance of using mentor texts when conferring with students about their writing. At the end of the session, a teacher raised her hand and said, "I need a list of twenty-five picture books you think I should read to my second graders and use in writing workshop."

I hesitated before answering: "I can give you a list, but why not spend a Saturday afternoon in the stacks of your local library exploring the picture books, finding ones you love and can use to teach writing?"

"I don't have the time," she said. "Just tell me what kinds of things I can teach from each of the books, and I'll use them."

At first, I felt frustrated she didn't want to find her own texts. A few hours later, I realized she might be unsure about how to find picture books worthy of adopting as mentor texts. Perhaps she'd never read like a writer and mined a picture book for teaching points before. My knee-jerk reaction led me to reflection, which reinforced the need for this book.

If you purchase the mentor texts I share in this book for your own classroom library, authors such as Matt de la Peña, Meg Medina, Seymour Simon, and Melissa Stewart will become your coteachers. Your students will learn to emulate author's craft and begin writing like Maribeth Boelts, Jen Bryant, Eve Bunting, and Mo Willems. My greatest hope is that you will want to go to the local library and get lost in the stacks for hours on end, plumbing picture books for craft moves. Finding your own gems is important if you want to cultivate a basket of mentor texts you adore. But if you're like that second-grade teacher, you might be unsure about what makes for a good mentor text. Let me share my selection process.

My Process

I want to fall in love when I'm reading books for the purpose of finding reading-writing connections. I always read for pleasure first. Although I'm subconsciously paying attention to the writing, I'm actually focusing on the characters and plot, if it's fiction, or on the new information I'm learning, if it's nonfiction. I'm concentrating on the quality of the illustrations, making sure the pictures are enhancing the story or the information being presented. After I fall in love, I ask myself if the book will be a good match to teach students something about writing. If so, I give it a second read.

This time, I'm reading like a writer. I'm looking for the way the author plays with language. I'm noticing the structure of the text. I'm listening for a distinct voice. However, I don't note any of my observations yet. By the third read of a book, I have sticky notes and a pen in hand so I can record the craft moves I notice, page by page (see Figure 1.1). At this point I paginate a book if it doesn't already have page numbers. I go online to find out how many pages the publisher says are in the book. Sometimes the publisher lists thirty-two pages, but I see only twenty-two pages of text. (That usually means the publisher is

Figure 1.1
I record craft moves I notice page by page as I read through the book a third time.

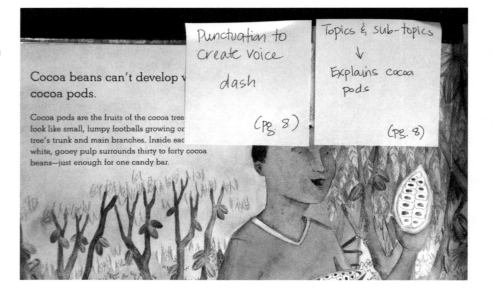

Figure 1.2
Each time I reread the book, I find more things I can teach young writers.

counting the front cover as page one, the front end paper as page two and so on, and the back cover as page thirty-two.)

I don't go through a book just once looking for craft moves. I read through it several times to make sure I have caught all the features I can teach a young writer (see Figure 1.2). Then I sort through the sticky notes to find craft moves that appear in at least two places in a text because it helps kids to see multiple examples if they're going to try them in their own writing.

Next, I sort my sticky notes by craft move on a piece of chart paper (see Figure 1.3). If I find only one sticky note for a particular craft move, I toss it. Then I create a Word document and include any craft move that appears two or more times in the text. From there, I explain why writers use a particular craft move and flesh out the points I want to teach in a lesson. I develop explanations and examples, as well as lines of inquiry, to use in small-group lessons. I always record the page numbers where I found the craft moves for easy reference. Sometimes I make notations about things I'd teach to sophisticated writers, such as a sentence-terminating period prior to ellipses. Also, I note places for additional supports I might give to inexperienced writers, such as retelling a story by moving their fingers across the text before writing it down on paper. Making notes about differentiation can also help because often my small-group strategy lessons morph into one-to-one mentor text conferences.

Figure 1.3
I use chart paper to track the craft moves I noticed in the text. Anything that appears once, like the single sticky note that originally appeared in the second row here, gets removed from my list of craft moves.

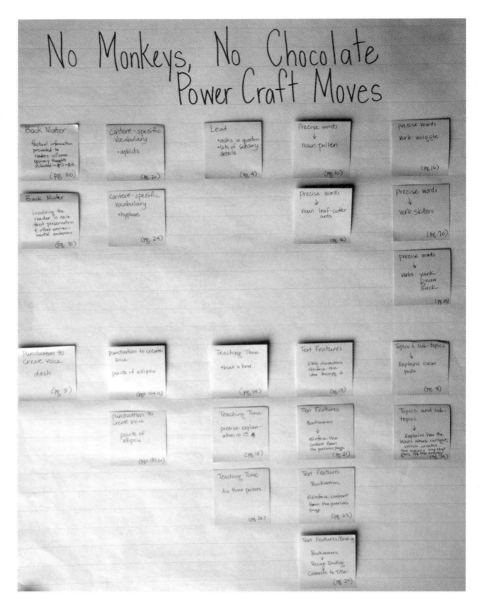

Working with Colleagues

It is often easier (and more fun!) to mine picture books for craft moves when you're working alongside colleagues. It helps to have someone else sitting next to you with whom you can share ideas. And later, you can draft small-group craft lessons with them using the books you found together.

You can also enlist the help of librarians in your school or at your local library in advance of your visit; they can assist you by pulling a variety of picture books. The friendly librarians at the East Shore Area Library in Harrisburg, Pennsylvania, once pulled *hundreds* of books for me, alphabetized them, and placed them on two rolling carts. They encouraged me to reserve a conference room, which was free, so the group of teachers I was working with could have a quiet space to read away from the children's section. A librarian can be your best friend when you're doing this kind of work.

Power Craft Moves

I don't think I learned to write by learning individual craft moves. Rather I learned to write by being blown away by books, by feeling their impact, and hoping I might impact a reader even 1/100th as much.

—Ralph Fletcher, personal conversation

Nearly every picture book could serve as a mentor text to help students become better writers. However, some books offer more value than others. Typically, I examine picture books through a lens based on the qualities of good writing: meaning, genre, structure, detail, voice, and conventions (Anderson 2005). Over the years I've come up with ten *power* craft moves for fiction and ten for nonfiction books, based on the things I hope to see in my students' writing, to help me determine what I can teach young writers from picture books (see Figure 1.4).

Figure 1.4
Craft moves we want all young writers to have in their toolboxes

Power Craft Moves	
Fiction Picture Books	**Nonfiction Picture Books**
Dialogue	Back Matter
Internal Thinking	Content-Specific Vocabulary
Lead/Ending	Lead/Ending
Punctuation to Create Voice	Precise Words
Repetition	Punctuation to Create Voice
Show, Don't Tell	Quotes and Sources
Specific Details	Repetition
Structure	Teaching Tone
Turning Point	Text Features
Varied Sentence Lengths	Topics and Subtopics

Every picture book I adopt as a mentor text needs to have at least six power craft moves. With six or more power craft moves, I can use each of the selected picture books in a variety of conferences and small-group lessons with inexperienced, mid-range, and sophisticated writers.

Teaching Craft Moves to Strengthen the Writer

When I confer with a young writer, I'm concerned about the child's writing being focused and detailed, not whether it includes similes or other grammar and punctuation features. So when I mine a picture book for craft moves, I rarely consider the author's use of figurative language because that's not the most pressing thing the majority of young writers need to work on. Figurative language can make a piece of writing sound better, but teaching kids how to insert it into their writing won't necessarily make them better writers.

During a professional development session with teachers in summer 2015, one teacher said "figurative language is kind of like the icing on the cake." As a cupcake lover, I liken figurative language to the decorations on top of a cupcake: they're great to have, but a cupcake is complete if it has a moist cake and sweet icing.

All kinds of figurative language—metaphors, personification, hyperbole, and so on—can make writing stronger. But deep figurative language instruction can wait until kids have a grade-level command of structure, development, and language conventions. During a writing conference with young students I am more concerned with what Carl Anderson calls the qualities of good writing. In *Assessing Writers,* he stresses that lifelong writers write well when they do the following:

- Communicate *meaning*
- Use *genre* knowledge
- *Structure* their writing
- Write with *detail*
- Give their writing *voice*
- Use *conventions* (2005, 58)

Similarly, I want students to communicate meaning in any piece of writing they craft. I want them to show evidence of the genre in which they're writing. I want them to use a structure that will help readers navigate the text. I want them to use a variety of details specific to the genre in which they're writing. I want them to carefully select words to make their writing come alive. And, obviously, I want kids to write with proper grammar, mechanics, and spelling. Because these qualities are so important to good writing, I have focused the strategy lessons in this book around these six areas.

Teaching Craft Moves to Apply Conventions

This book doesn't have lessons to teach grammar rules to students. Although writing is more powerful when it's properly punctuated and correctly spelled, I don't consider conventions as craft moves. Instead, you'll find lessons that use power craft moves to apply writing conventions, such as *using punctuation to create voice* and *varied sentence lengths*. We want our young writers to learn how to use punctuation from mentor texts in a purposeful way as they compose, revise, and edit their writing.

Dan Feigelson interviewed author and illustrator Natalie Babbit in his book *Practical Punctuation: Lessons on Rule Making and Rule Breaking in Elementary Writing* (2008). Feigelson asked Babbit why she used lots of dashes in *Tuck Everlasting*. She said she considered dashes to be like stage directions. "It's just a way to read it. You know, pause and then go on, then pause again and go on. It gives you time to think about what you're reading" (203). Babbit's thoughts have stuck with me for years. They've allowed me to think of punctuation differently; I started to see the marks on the page as tools writers could use purposefully to tell readers how to interact with the text. We want our young writers to have a say in the way readers interpret their writing. It's also important to teach students to be intentional about punctuation because it gives their writing voice.

As M. Colleen Cruz says, "If you have a text—you have a grammar mentor" (2015, 92). We can point out the ways published authors vary their sentence lengths to add cadence to their writing or to slow their readers down and focus on important details. In addition, we can invite our students to do an inquiry alongside us so we can discover how an author punctuates dialogue or uses ellipsis points.

The Value of Picture Books Across Grade Levels

Some teachers believe picture books are for little kids. I disagree. Although I used excerpts from middle grades novels to demonstrate the qualities of good writing to my fourth- and fifth-grade students, I usually selected picture books as writing workshop mentor text. Picture books are

- *Short*—You can read them quickly and then use them to demonstrate a strategy during a mini-lesson or conference.
- *Visual*—The illustrations support all students, including struggling readers and English language learners, with comprehension.
- *Engaging*—Many kids have become disengaged or reluctant readers by the time they reach fourth grade. Picture books are a way to invite them back to reading. Using picture books as mentor texts can help marginalized readers make better independent reading selections because they see that their teacher values picture books.
- *Community builders*—Picture books provide an accessible way to tackle tough topics, which students can discuss at length in the classroom. Kids can often relate to the struggles of the characters in the picture books and are more willing to discuss or write about those struggles because they've seen them portrayed on the pages of a picture book.
- *Anchors*—Students can use beloved picture books as touchstones in their reading and writing work. The most memorable books can be used across a school year.

Many outstanding middle and high school educators—including prominent bloggers, authors, and speakers such as Sarah Mulhern Gross, Paul Hankins, Cindy Minnich, and Pernille Ripp—also use picture books with their secondary students, for the reasons I mentioned previously and also because they provide high-level opportunities for inference and interpretation work, as well as spark empathy and ignite creativity. Picture books are a powerful resource at any grade level!

You may look at some of the featured picture books and think, "that's not a fit for my grade level." Some books, like *Knuffle Bunny Free* and *The Slug,* lend themselves more to primary grades, whereas *Founding Mothers* and *Happy Like Soccer* might be a perfect fit with upper elementary students. You know your students best. I'm confident you'll find several appropriate mentor texts from the twenty books I've included in Chapters 5 and 6.

Authors You Love and Trust Are the Best Mentors

Authors are like trusted colleagues we invite to teach alongside us. Their books inspire us, their personal stories and struggles resonate with us, and they show us new ways of understanding. We welcome authors we trust into our classrooms to help us teach our students strategies that will help them become better writers.

Look to the authors whose books you love. Their stories are the ones you want to read to your kids over and over and over again. Their books serve multiple purposes, can be used across genres, and demonstrate many different qualities of good writing. They might even make themselves available for free Skype sessions (Messner 2009) or answer questions from students on Twitter. But most of all, the best mentors are those whom you trust to teach alongside you, day after day.

This book can be a springboard for you and your students to work together as you study mentor texts and learn from them. To find the best mentors for your students, get to know the authors as well as their books. Sit down and read through the books on the shelves of your classroom library with the intent to use them for multiple purposes. Figure 1.5 poses some questions you can ask about a book or an author as you search for mentor authors and mentor texts.

Figure 1.5

Some questions you can ask about a book or an author as you search for mentor authors and mentor texts

About a book	About an author
• What's this book about? How will this book help my students write about a topic?	• Is this an author I know and trust or is he or she new to me?

• What genre of writing does this book fall into?
  • How will this book help me teach a given genre to my students?
  • What genre-specific things can I teach from this text?
	• Are there other books by this author I can use as mentor texts? If so, where can I use them in my curriculum?

• How many craft moves can I explain to my students with this book?	• Does this author have a website where she or he shares information about her- or himself as a writer?
• Will I be able to use this book when I confer with inexperienced writers, mid-range writers, and sophisticated writers?	• Does this author answer student questions via mail or e-mail or use social media to interact with his or her readers?

Learning to Read Mentor Texts

Now that we've discussed some ways to select picture books as mentor texts and identify power craft moves used by our favorite authors, let's look at how we can set the stage for reading picture books. In the next chapter, we will see how read-aloud time can become a cherished part of the school day during which we can model comprehension strategies, cultivate classroom community, and share the connections among reading, writing, listening, and speaking.

Chapter 2

Reading Picture Books for Pleasure and Purpose

Picture books are ideal for reading to elementary students. They deliver a full story in a short amount of time, thanks to the way in which most authors economize their word count. There is something magical about gathering children together on the classroom rug to read a well-crafted story with beautiful illustrations. Read-aloud time becomes an anticipated time of day when children know that their teacher will read books that engage them or teach them new things while dazzling their senses with beautiful pictures.

We want to choose read-aloud books that serve a purpose. Because of the pressures of preparing students for high-stakes tests and standards requirements, many teachers rarely read aloud a book *just for fun*. Yet, as Lucy Calkins notes, "It's the books we've read and reread, savored and shared that will affect us as writers" (Calkins 1994, 277). It's my belief that if we give students at least one read-through of a picture book with a few interactions, such as turn and talks, stop and jots, and stop and thinks, they will come to appreciate the book and will usually adopt it as a beloved mentor text.

The Power of Story

Let me confess this to you now, dear colleague. I have cried during read-aloud on several occasions. The first time I ever cried in front of my class was during Chapter 14 of *Kira-Kira* by Cynthia Kadohata. This is the point in the book where readers learn that no one was by Lynn's side when she died of lymphoma. Lynn, the teenage sister of the book's protagonist, found beauty in everything. The notion of dying alone, without being surrounded by loved ones, overwhelmed me. Although I had read the book independently prior to reading it to my class, I was overcome with emotion when I read this section aloud. I paused. I swallowed. Tears pricked my eyelashes. I began to cry. I blotted my tears away and tried to keep reading, but then I noticed that several of my fifth graders were shedding tears too. And the kids who weren't sobbing were consoling the kids (and me) who were. Our sob fest was barely two minutes old when the school principal walked into the room for his daily check-in. He quickly and quietly left the room so my kids and I could work through our emotions as a class.

I tell you this story because I want you to know that reading aloud to your students can be powerful. *Kira-Kira* is a chapter book we spent a few weeks reading, rather than a picture book finished in a day. In either case, read-alouds can build classroom community. Once children become comfortable with the basics of respectful and purposeful school talk—using conversational prompts so that talk sounds genuine, listening to others, disagreeing respectfully, and growing thinking based on other people's ideas—they can use read-aloud time to tackle tough subjects together and express honest emotions.

One Book, Many Purposes

> *In the mini-lesson before our writing workshop, we will often return to texts we've introduced during the morning read-aloud (or during a later read-aloud of a chapter), this time to study passages we love, to talk about what the author has done, and to consider the effect the author was hoping to create. We will probably not reread the book in its entirety for this discussion.*
>
> —Lucy Calkins (2001)

There's *never* enough time when you're a classroom teacher. In a week filled with an end-of-unit celebration, a field trip, or a special guest visit, you may feel pressured to sacrifice your shared read-aloud time. Instead, try to find mentor books that can do double or triple duty in your lessons. It helps to find books you can revisit during reading and writing mini-lessons or content-areas periods. Let's look at a few examples.

Across Units of Study

It's ideal to use picture books across multiple units of study in writing workshop. Children become familiar with mentor texts when they use them throughout the school year. The authors of texts revisited in multiple units of study also become our students' guides to good writing. We talk with students about "the way Candace Fleming used descriptive language" or "the way Mo Willems made us laugh." It's almost as if these authors, whose books we've studied with our students multiple times, are teaching alongside us.

From Read-Aloud to Workshops

The natural connection between reading and writing and listening and oral language are very visible in picture books.
—Lester Laminack and Reba Wadsworth (2006)

At several points during the school year we find ourselves teaching related units in both reading and writing workshop. One October I taught a unit of study about character during reading workshop at the same time that my students were writing personal narratives. It becomes easier to connect the read-aloud book to reading and writing workshop when students write in a matching genre. I might use the book I read aloud in the morning as a demonstration text in both my reading and writing mini-lessons.

A word of caution: when books start pulling quadruple duty—morning read-aloud book, interactive read-aloud text, demonstration text for mini-lessons, and go-to book for vocabulary sessions—you run the risk of overusing them. Although it helps to maximize your read-aloud choices, don't oversaturate students by focusing too much on one particular book.

From Read-Aloud to Content-Area Writing

I always sought out interesting trade books when I taught nonfiction reading to my students. It was important for me to identify high-interest books for read-alouds because I used them as demonstration texts in mini-lessons.

The same thing should be true of the books we hold up to our students as mentor texts when we teach informational writing in writing workshop or in the content areas. If we want our students to write strong informational pieces, we must provide exemplar texts, some of which can be picture books. Appendix A of the Common Core State Standards describes numerous types of informational writing children can craft:

Informational/explanatory writing includes a wide array of genres, including academic genres such as literary analyses, scientific and historical reports, summaries, and précis writing as well as forms of workplace and functional writing such as instructions, manuals, memos, reports, applications, and resumes. As students advance through the grades, they expand their repertoire of informational/explanatory genres and use them effectively in a variety of disciplines and domains. (NGA/CCSSO 2010, 23)

With so many kinds of informational writing, it is possible to teach the qualities of good writing from many of the same nonfiction picture books we use during read-aloud sessions.

Immersing Students in Mentor Texts

It's wise to spend a few days immersing students in the genre in which they are going to write (Bomer 2010; Caine 2008; Eickholdt 2015; Ray 2006). Engaging with good writing helps kids develop a vision for their own texts. For some units of study, the best mentor texts are those written by other kids, such as exemplary work from another teacher's class or writing you have collected from former students. In addition, for many units of study you can provide students with picture books to give them a sense of the genre.

Here's how a writing workshop immersion day might go:

9:00–9:20: Whole-class reading and discussion
9:20–9:40: Partner work
9:40–9:50: Independent writing time
9:50–10:00: Share session

Whole-class Reading and Discussion: Select one of the picture books you're planning to use as a mentor text. Read it aloud to your students during your regularly scheduled read-aloud time so they can process the information. Next, read it again, this time asking students to notice the craft or, rather, how it's written. After reading the book aloud for craft, work with your students to record what they admired and noticed when listening to the text a second time (Fletcher 2011). Katherine Bomer (2010) suggests describing what the writer is doing in simple, nonliterary terms. Some students might remark on key features of the genre, whereas others might notice the effect the words had on them. All responses should be honored and recorded on an anchor chart, which can be used as a reference. Reading aloud to students and spending time discussing what you noticed will go a long way to making students' independent work on an immersion day meaningful. Finally, set up the partner work students will do once they leave the meeting area.

Partner Work: Students work with partners to read picture books as writers do. You might let student teams look through a few picture books and have conversations about what they notice. Another idea is providing a guide that students can use to learn how to read like a writer (see Figure 2.1).

Figure 2.1
Use this form to help students, especially those who are new to using picture books as mentor texts.

Name: _____ **Date:** _____

Title of Picture Book: _____

Author: _____

Illustrator (if different than author): _____

Topic: _____ **Genre:** _____

Type of Illustrations: _____

DIRECTIONS:

1. Read the picture book.
2. Answer these questions.
   a. What did you like about this picture book? Be specific.

   b. Did the author do anything you admire? That is, were there parts you read more than once because you liked the way they were written? (That's craft!)

   c. What might you call the craft moves the author used? Name them!

   d. Have you seen other authors use these craft moves before? If so, who? Where?

   e. How did using these craft moves make this book more interesting or easy to read?

   f. How did this picture book inspire you as a writer?

   g. How will you try to use these craft moves in your own writing?

This form was based on the work of Katie Wood Ray.

Although I believe such a guide can provide a nice scaffold for students who are learning to notice and note the craft of good writers, I do not recommend asking students to fill out worksheets on a regular basis. Once students become comfortable discussing mentor texts, they will develop their own record-keeping systems to track things they admire and notice in a text. Encourage students to use these forms as resources they can refer to during a unit of study. If we teach students how to take notes about what they notice in mentor texts, they will likely return to books they admired when they need inspiration.

Independent Writing Time: Most of your students will be inspired to write after reading picture books on immersion days. Provide time for them to write—even if it's only for ten minutes—on these occasions.

Share Session: Make time for students to share what they learned by closely reading picture books, as writers do, on immersion days. Experiment with different methods of sharing, such as a "whip-style" share (Ayres and Shubitz 2010, 155) where every person or team shares something quickly with the class, or more intimate conversations where partners discuss what they discovered. There are many possibilities for share time (Murphy 2014). See Figure 2.2 for more ideas. Be sure to leave enough time for students to learn from each other's discoveries on immersion days.

Maximize Your Time with Predictable Structures and Procedures

Now that you're confident about the ways you can use picture books, let's think about classroom management. The lessons in this book can only happen if you have systems in place to make sure your kids are doing what they're supposed to be doing at all points during the workshop. In Chapter 3, we will see how creating special writing workshop expectations, developing a predictable workshop rhythm, teaching students how to be responsible for classroom supplies, and timing yourself can provide you with the time you need to meet with as many students as possible during independent writing time, which should be the heart of your writing workshop.

Whole-Class Share	Everyone gets a turn to share. This works well for a product share when the content will be only a few words, such as a title or a single line from a piece of writing. It helps to give the listeners an active role. The listeners can sit, notebooks in hand, ready to write down any tidbit they would like to use in future writing.
Turn and Talk	Talk to a partner. This is a nice alternative to the whole class share. Everyone still gets a turn to share, but with a partner instead of the whole class.
Anchor Chart	Record the day's learning on a classroom chart. This is a concrete way to link back to the mini-lesson and reflect on the day's work. Rather than creating an anchor chart during the mini-lesson, save it for share time after students have had a chance to try their hand at the day's lesson.
Thumbs Up/ Thumbs Down	Restate the learning target for the day and have kids rate themselves as writers. For example, you could say, "Today we learned that writers sometimes use pictures to add detail to their writing. Think about yourself as a writer today. Thumbs up if your picture added detail, thumbs down if it didn't, and thumbs to the side if you're not sure." This only takes a minute to accomplish, but it encourages students to reflect on themselves as writers, and it gives you a quick reading of the class.
Reflective Questions	Ask students to think about themselves as writers. Examples: "What did you learn about yourself as a writer today?" "What did you try as a writer today?" "What did you struggle with as a writer today?" Everyone can share with a partner, a few students can share with the whole class, or everyone can simply sit quietly and think.
Teacher Choice	Strategically choose one or two students to share their process or product. Choose students who did an exemplary job of meeting the day's learning target or who took risks as writers. The students share their work or their thinking as writers, and share time becomes another opportunity to reinforce a teaching point.
Written Response	Instead of sharing orally, students can quickly reflect in writing on a sticky note or an exit ticket. This is helpful for the teacher who needs to do a whole-class assessment of the day's work or plan small-group work for the following day.
Go Digital	Use technology to share. Students can tweet out a reflection at the end of writing workshop or contribute to a class Google document.

Figure 2.2
Literacy coach Dana Murphy compiled a list of share session possibilities for writing workshop, which she shared on the Two Writing Teachers website in 2014.

Chapter

3 Establishing Routines and Procedures for Writing with Mentor Texts

I know school scheduling can be wonky. Kids get pulled in and out of your classroom. Assemblies can distort the balance of a day. Snow days can wreak havoc on an entire week! Despite all the disruptions to your schedule, it's important to set aside a chunk of time to devote to writing *at least* four of the five days of the school week. Students need regular opportunities to practice writing and work within a community of writers. They must exercise their writing muscles to get stronger. As Katie Wood Ray asserts, "If writing workshops aren't happening daily, it's hard for children to learn that aspect of writing. So, really, the regular-ness of it is very important" (2008).

Examine your schedule closely and, if necessary, work with your administrators to find the time for four or five writing workshop slots, each forty-five to sixty minutes long, during each school week. If you make writing a priority in your schedule, it will happen daily. (Except on those occasional field trip days!)

In addition to a regular schedule for writing, you will need to establish routines for managing time, materials, and assignments. It's crucial to have procedures in place so your writing workshop will function like a well-oiled machine. Let's take a look at a few key procedures in more detail.

Create a List of Expectations

It helps to have expectations for writing workshop. These special "rules," compiled by you and your students, will keep the classroom running smoothly and prepare students for group work, independent writing, and transitions. To generate expectations for your writing workshop, encourage students to think about issues that may arise when they work together or alone. Consider the following when formulating questions you will ask your students:

- Why should they write pieces that hold meaning or value to them?
- How can they use their voices to share ideas and opinions in a respectful way?
- How will they maintain their focus during independent writing time?
- What does accountable partner work look like?
- How should a productive and respectful share session look and sound? (Shubitz 2012)

Discuss Noise Level

Some professional writers find writing to a background of noise conducive to their creative process, but many children need a quiet space in which to create. Ask students about their preferences and decide which noise levels are appropriate. Many teachers use soft music such as tunes from Enya or Yo-Yo Ma to transition students from the meeting area to their focus spots. Once the music stops, many teachers require ten minutes of silent writing time. From there, the rest of independent writing time can include soft voices so that peers can confer with one another while those who need quiet have a reasonably peaceful environment in which to write.

Build Stamina

It's necessary to build stamina in students so they'll have the patience to write and revise *every* day during independent writing time. Students who are young or are new to writing workshop will have to build up to forty-five minutes of independent writing time. I suggest increasing independent writing time in five-minute increments. When I taught fourth grade, we spent just ten minutes writing independently during the first few days of school. After a few days, we wrote for fifteen minutes. By the sixth week of school, we were engaged in independent writing for forty-five minutes.

Even the youngest writers can work for up to forty-five minutes. Betsy Hubbard challenges her kindergartners and first graders to increase their stamina during independent writing time by using quiet voices and working throughout the entire writing workshop (2013). She tracks their progress in five-minute increments (see Figure 3.1).

Figure 3.1
Young writers can build stamina over time.

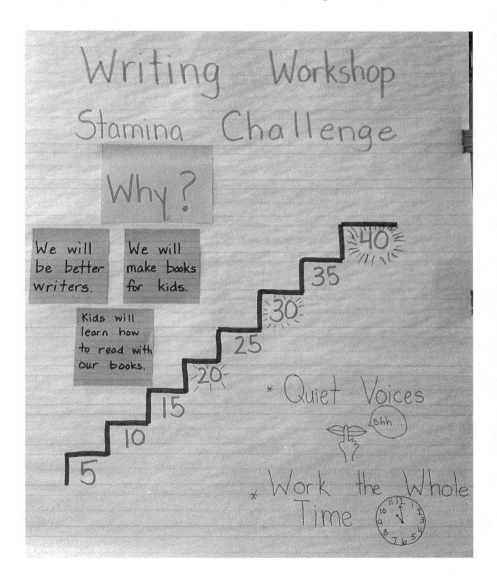

Develop a Flow

Writing workshop usually begins with a ten- to fifteen-minute mini-lesson. I suggest closing each mini-lesson by asking students to create a plan, verbal or written depending on their age, for how they will utilize their independent writing time (Ayres and Shubitz 2010). Then students can head off to their focus spots (Ayres and Shubitz 2010) for independent writing time, which makes up the bulk of writing workshop. Ideally, independent writing time will last for forty-five minutes, which provides plenty of time to confer with small groups of students for strategy lessons. Each workshop concludes with a share session that lasts five to ten minutes.

Get Unstuck

It's important to address what students can do if they find themselves off track during the first weeks of the school year. "We want our students to become independent so they can work through rough patches in their writing when they get stuck. This means we must give students the space they need to work through the hard parts even when it looks like they're not working at all" (Ayres and Shubitz 2010, 13). Kids need strategies to help them work through the tough parts of the writing process so they won't throw up their hands and declare they have writer's block when they should be working.

One of my former students loved to claim he had writer's block as a way to avoid writing. I created a "No Writer's Block Zone," which eliminated that excuse from his repertoire (see Figure 3.2). By eradicating writer's block as an excuse, I was able to get to the heart of the

Figure 3.2
Many kids have heard of writer's block and will employ it as an excuse for why they cannot write. A sign like this reminds kids that they need to find ways to help themselves get unstuck rather than claiming they have a case of writer's block.

problem every time he got stuck. Students need to know how to move forward so they don't disrupt you or their peers during independent writing time.

Come Prepared

Get students into the habit of bringing their writing samples and a writing utensil to a strategy lesson. Primary-grade writers might bring their writing folders with stapled booklets, whereas intermediate-grades writers might bring their writer's notebooks or drafts. You might wish to rehearse this process using interactive modeling (Wilson 2012) during the first weeks of the school year.

Use a conferring toolkit for your conferences and strategy lessons. Items you might wish to keep in your conferring toolkit include:

- mentor texts
- record-keeping forms (handwritten or electronic)
- checklists or rubrics
- mini-charts
- your writer's notebook
- supplies (markers, pens, sticky notes, loose-leaf paper, and index cards)

Having a well-stocked toolkit close at hand will keep you focused on your students during each strategy lesson. A well-stocked toolkit also enables you to be mobile. Rather than conducting strategy lessons in the same spot daily, you can move around the classroom with your toolkit, which you could carry in a canvas tote bag or a zippered, three-ring binder. Figure 3.3 shows

Figure 3.3
A record-keeping form such as this is an essential part of a well-stocked toolkit for conferring with students.

Strategy Lesson Log				
Date	**Students Present**	**Power Craft Move**	**Teaching Point**	**Demonstration Text**

one version of a record-keeping form that you could use to monitor students' progress.

Consider Communal Supplies

Provide students with access to all the supplies they will need during independent writing time (see Figure 3.4). Supply caddies—stocked with pens, crayons, markers, scissors, and glue sticks—can be placed on clusters of desks or tables during independent writing time. You can also set up a writing center containing items all students might need in a central classroom location. Use interactive modeling to show students how to responsibly access, use, and care for the communal supplies in the supply caddies and in the writing center.

Figure 3.4
A writing center may contain a variety of paper, index cards, sticky notes, clipboards, interesting writing utensils, paper clips, tape, and dictionaries.

Make Mentor Texts Available

Ideally, you'll have several copies of each picture book you use. Realistically, this is challenging because picture books can be pricey. Carl Anderson suggests a middle ground. He writes: "It's a good idea to give students copies of texts the class has read and studied. Then, during conferences, we can ask them to bring out their copy of the piece we want to discuss with them. Isoke Nia, one of my colleagues at the Reading and Writing Project, has a wonderful name for these hand-outs: 'literary gifts.' When I pass out literary gifts, I ask students to put them into their writing folders or to tape them onto a page in their writers notebooks" (2000, 134).

Sometimes copyright laws prohibit us from disseminating these "literary gifts" to students. In those cases Anderson suggests that "we can make a few bound sets of student texts (or write for permission to duplicate copyrighted material) and put them in the classroom library, the writing materials center, or in baskets on each table in the class-room. Or instead of binding the texts, we can laminate a few copies of each one" (2000, 135).

Regardless of how you do it, make the mentor texts accessible to students so they can look to them for ideas or inspiration any time during writing workshop.

Minimize Disruptions

It's important for all your students to know they cannot interrupt you—unless it's an emergency—while you're leading a writing confer-ence or small-group strategy lesson. Teach students to wait until the conclusion of your small-group lesson to ask a question. Many teachers wear a visual conferring reminder (e.g., a hat, scarf, or sweater) to tell students *not* to interrupt them while they're conferring or meeting with a small group.

If students need help while you're meeting with small groups, encourage them to eavesdrop on your strategy lesson. Often children will hear something that will help them when they listen to the working talk of other writers. And if they don't, then at least they'll have spent some time learning a strategy they can add to their writing toolbox!

Label stackable trays by subject area and put them in places where students can turn in their work. This will minimize disruptions if students finish their books or drafts during independent writing time. Leave a stapler next to the stackable tray so students can put their "final" product together (Ayres and Shubitz 2010) rather than enlisting your help.

Watch the Time

Limit the length of each small-group lesson. Anything more than ten minutes defeats the purpose of meeting with students in highly individualized strategy groups. In five to ten minutes, you should be able to teach one strategy, study the text, and then transfer it to students' own writing. Allow students to have a go with the strategy you taught. Then send them off to finish independently what they worked on with you. Use a stopwatch that counts *up,* rather than a timer that beeps, to keep track of time while delivering small-group lessons. If you find yourself at the four-minute mark and you haven't allowed students to try out the strategy in their writing, then speed up your teaching.

Move into Groups

With the procedures mentioned in this chapter in mind, you can run your writing workshop smoothly. In Chapter 4, we will focus on successful strategies for small-group instruction during writing workshop. I'll help you discover a variety of ways to form small groups of students that may meet once or for a series of several lessons to help them reach a goal.

4

Chapter

Small-Group Strategy Lessons: Talking with Students About Their Writing

Although we know teachers should confer with every student at least once a week, most of us can't find the time. I know this not only from my work as a consultant who helps teachers learn to confer, but also because I taught classes that ranged from eighteen to thirty-two students. It was impossible to confer weekly with each of my thirty-two fifth graders, unless I had a student teacher in the room, because I only had thirty minutes of independent writing time that particular year. I could meet with a maximum of six students in a day—and that was if there weren't any "fires" to put out. In order to meet with every student at least once a week, I began using more strategy lessons, grouping peers who were demonstrating the same needs.

The small-group lessons in this book are based on the work of Lucy Calkins and her colleagues at the Teachers College Reading and Writing Project. In *The Art of Teaching Reading,* Calkins writes:

> *In a strategy lesson, we again work with a small (although sometimes a large) group of readers and we usually have a shared text. We teach a strategy, usually by demonstrating it and then we scaffold readers as they try that strategy, helping them become increasingly independent with it. Later, we observe to see whether the tool we taught has become part of*

each reader's ongoing repertoire. Strategy lessons are rather like small-group mini-lessons in the middle of the reading workshop. (2001, 44)

Strategy lessons used during writing workshop take place during independent writing time and are based on the issues you notice (see Figure 4.1). Because groups are heterogeneous and consist of three to five children, the instruction is highly individualized. We might choose to begin a strategy lesson with a compliment for the entire group and then launch into a teaching point. After demonstrating how to use a strategy, we give students a long time to try out the strategy in their own writing.

Although there's a high level of teacher talk in a strategy lesson, kids have to do most of the work. As teachers, we have to be careful not to overscaffold. Instead, we need to provide students with just enough support to become independent so they can practice the skill repeatedly and then transfer it to other types of writing.

Figure 4.1
An overview of a strategy lesson, which takes place during independent writing time

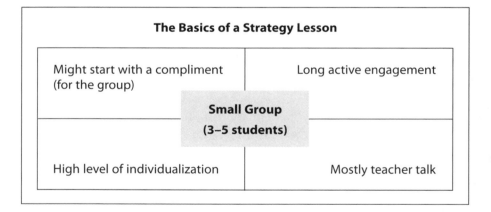

A Word of Caution

Small-group strategy lessons are *not* a substitute for one-to-one conferences. Although it seems easier to meet with groups of students than to confer with them individually, you won't develop rich writer-to-writer relationships if you meet with children only in small groups. For example, you may choose to compliment the group, but you aren't building up each child with specific compliments if you only lead strategy lessons.

IDEAL: If your schedule permits, I suggest pulling students for at least one strategy lesson per week in addition to one-to-one writing conferences *or* partner conferences. This enables you to meet each child's needs while maximizing your time during independent writing.

REASONABLE: If the size of your class and a limited amount of time for writing workshop make it impossible for you to meet with all of your students one to one every week, then meet with each student for a small-group strategy lesson every week and confer with every child at least every other week.

Forming Groups

Your small groups can consist of inexperienced, mid-range, and sophisticated writers who are demonstrating the same need on a given day. It's important to be flexible with your groupings because they are not meant to become stagnant. Rather, they should be temporary and task specific.

There are several ways to form small groups for strategy lessons:

Take Cues from Students: If you notice that a few students don't understand what's asked of them during the active engagement portion of your mini-lesson, pull them into a small-group lesson before independent writing time begins.

Read Plan Boxes: This end-of-mini-lesson check-in enables you to see what your students' intentions are for their independent writing time. Keep a sticky note and pen by your side as you read students' plan boxes. Jot the names of students with similar needs. You can create dynamic groups based on the needs your students communicate in their daily plan.

Read Student Writing: Create small groups for strategy lessons based on your students' writing samples.
  - *Use On-Demand Writing:* Study pre- and post-assessment writing from students, including quick-publish or on-demand pieces. After you read through the class's writing, you'll want to align it to grade-level expectations, such as the Common Core State Standard's English Language Arts Standards or the Teachers College Reading and Writing Project's Learning Progressions. Next, sort students' writing into piles. Look for strengths and next steps. For example, you might place sticky notes to indicate things the students did well as writers and

what they might do to move to the next level. Then, make a list of goals for your students based on their needs. Finally, group students into small groups based on the next steps you identified, such as crafting leads and endings or writing with strings of detail.

- *Study Students' Notebooks:* Regularly checking writer's notebooks can help you form small groups too. During a unit of study, there are usually a few days set aside for students to collect writing from the genre. They choose a seed idea and then spend a few days nurturing it in their notebooks before starting to draft. Study the writing students compose at home or during the collecting and nurturing days of a unit. If you notice that several students need the same type of teaching—creating a new paragraph every time there is a new speaker, for example, or focusing on one idea per entry—you can teach them a strategy lesson rather than conferring with them separately.

- *Read Drafts:* I used to read every student's draft multiple times during a unit of study. I came to realize this was an inefficient method of review. Eventually, I began selecting a handful of students' drafts to read during each cycle.

  You can read half the class's drafts and make note of commonalities. If three to five students have the same need, form a group and teach a strategy lesson. If all the drafts you read reflect the same issue, then teach that strategy as a whole-class mini-lesson.

  Be sure to track whose draft you have read during each cycle. This will ensure that you're reading all your students' drafts over time.

Focus on Goals: Many teachers have three to five writing goals for every student, which they create based on reading their students' writing and then conferring with them. If you need to meet with a group of students over time, teach a series of small-group lessons to them.

- *Qualities of Good Writing:* You might choose to focus some of your students' writing goals, such as elaboration or structure, through targeted, small-group strategy lessons (see Figure 4.2). Look across your students' writing goals to identify commonalities. Meet with the same three to five students on a regular basis until they attain the goal.

Figure 4.2

Planning for small-group instruction is based on students' writing goals. Look across your students' writing goals to find goals multiple students have in common. Write them in the left column. Decide on the mentor texts you'll use to strengthen this writing quality in your students. Finally, craft teaching points for each goal (use the lesson sets to help).

- *Grammar Related:* Set at least one grammar-related goal for each student. Group students who have the same goal and meet with them over the course of a few weeks. For instance, you might have three students who need to vary their punctuation. You can gather those students together for small-group strategy lessons weekly until they have mastered using exclamation points, question marks, periods, and ellipses in their writing. Perhaps you have another group of young writers who are ready to experiment with dashes instead of only using commas. Meet with those students every couple of weeks for a strategy lesson that deals with varying their punctuation.

Writing Goal/Quality	Students Who Need Help with This	Mentor Texts	Teaching Points
FOCUS: Establish focus in leads	Aerin Colton Josh Sara	*A Splash of Red* *No Monkeys, No Chocolate* *Trouper* *Yard Sale*	1. Writers craft leads that tell more than where the writing takes place. Some writers develop a sense of era by helping readers understand when their narrative takes place. Writers can create a sense of era by using dates and describing events happening at that time. 2. Many writers find it helps to open their writing with questions because they engage the reader. 3. Writers hook their readers by sharing a secret with them from the very start of their story. 4. Writers create a vivid image of the place where their story is set by including rich descriptions of it with their words.

Teaching Small Groups

Columbia University's Teachers College Reading and Writing Project recommends four types of instruction for writing workshop: demonstration, guided practice, explanation and example, and inquiry. Lucy Calkins (2013) likens the four methods for teaching writing to the way adults teach young children how to put on their shoes. Demonstrating would include narrating a step-by-step process for putting on shoes. For guided practice, an adult would help a child go through the process of putting on shoes while also providing directions of what to do with each foot and each shoe as they go along. For explanation and example, the adult might give the child a lecture about how to put on the shoe by telling and possibly showing the child how to do it. The adult might share some tips along the way, but overall, there's a lot of prep work the adult must do to make sure the verbal explanation and visual examples of putting on shoes makes sense. Finally, for inquiry, the adult might ask the child to figure out how the shoe got on his foot. The adult would ask questions to engage the child until he could accurately explain how he got the shoe on his foot.

Figure 4.3 shows how I apply all four methods of instruction recommended by Teachers College to mentor texts. You will notice all these elements in the lesson sets featured in this book. However, most of the small-group craft lessons I've included show explanation and example. You will name a craft move for students and show them how the authors made the move in their books. Then, you will invite students to practice the craft move in their own writing. Although some students might need you to "whisper in"—to provide them with lean-in prompts or immediate feedback—while they're writing, most will be able to try out the technique on their own because you will have shown them at least two examples from the text.

Figure 4.3
This chart shows how to apply the Teachers College Reading and Writing Project's recommended instruction for writing workshop to mentor texts.

Demonstration:	Guided Practice:	Explanation and Example:	Inquiry:
Teachers show students how to try out a craft move in a step-by-step manner.	Teachers coach students using lean-in prompts as they try out a craft move in their own writing.	Teachers show students an example of a craft move an author made and provide an explanation of how to make that move.	Teachers invite students to study a text with them, which enables students to discover the craft, name what they noticed, and transfer it to their own writing.

Power Craft Moves in Action

The small-group lessons in this book are designed to help you teach three to five students a power craft move so they can become stronger writers. The lessons are suggestive, not scripted. First and foremost, the small-group lessons should be based on the skills and strategies you want your students to master as writers. You may form dynamic groups of students who demonstrate the same writing need. However, some explanations and examples lend themselves better to inexperienced writers, whereas some are more appropriate for sophisticated writers. Figure 4.4 includes some prompts and questions that you can use to help frame your small-group lessons.

In each lesson, I name the craft move and provide a short rationale for why writers should employ it. I also list page numbers in each book

Figure 4.4

Prompts and short questions can help you frame small-group lessons for your students.

Gather the group:
- I want to compliment you. Some people are doing _____, but you're doing _____.
- You're doing smart work as writers. I see you _____.
- I noticed the way you're _____.

Set up the lesson:
- Today I want to teach you _____.
- Today we're going to study (title of book) together.
- Many writers find it helps to _____ because _____.

Teach the power craft move:
- Watch as I show you how (this author) did _____.
- Let's study the text together.
- Did you notice how (the author) was able to _____?
- Anytime you want to (name the strategy) you can try out (this craft move) in your writing.

Engage your students:
- I'd like you to try _____ while we're still together.
- I want you to try _____ on your own.

Connect to the work students do independently:
- So today and any day you're . . .
- You can add this to your writer's toolbox anytime you want to . . .
- When you go back to your focus spot, . . .
- Keep going!

---

where an author made each craft move so you can reread the text to your students. Revisiting specific sections of the books will not only refresh students' memory, but will also help them tap into the power of mentor texts. Every lesson includes an active engagement that invites students to try out the craft move you explained or studied alongside them.

The Tricky Business of Leads and Endings

Most, but not all, of the lesson sets in this book include lessons for leads and endings. I intentionally chose to omit a lead or an ending lesson if I didn't feel it would be particularly useful to teach young children (e.g., a lead or an ending may have relied heavily on an illustration). For example, I think Mo Willems, the author of *Knuffle Bunny Free: An Unexpected Diversion,* is brilliant! But as I thought about using the book to model how to write effective leads and endings, I imagined receiving stacks of published stories that would begin, "One day, not so long ago . . ." and end with, "And that is how . . . ." I didn't want students to use formulaic leads or endings.

Lynne Dorfman, coauthor of *Mentor Texts* (Dorfman and Cappelli 2007) and *Nonfiction Mentor Texts* (Dorfman and Cappelli 2009), shared tips about leads and endings that have helped me revise the way I think about teaching students to write them:

- Leads aren't always the first sentence of a book. Leads can be the first paragraph or first couple of pages of a picture book. Similarly, an ending isn't just the final line of the text. A picture book's ending might happen on the last few pages of the book.
- We want children to see that there are a variety of ways to open and close a text. We also want students to try out different leads and endings and then decide which one works best.
- Authors often use more than one strategy to introduce or close a text. As a result, it's perfectly fine for young writers to combine two types of leads. As you'll see, there are quite a few books with leads I describe as combinations of more than one type. See, for example, *A Splash of Red* and *Eat, Leo! Eat!*
- Similarly, some books might combine more than one type of ending. *Last Stop on Market Street* and *See What a Seal Can Do* are good examples of this approach. Noticing and naming this approach alongside students will help them learn how to craft

endings that are more complex. Although I used many lead and ending names from *Mentor Texts* (Dorfman and Cappelli 2007) and *Nonfiction Mentor Texts* (Dorfman and Cappelli 2009), I also invented names for some of the leads and endings I encountered (e.g., in *Big Red Kangaroo* and *Yard Sale*).

The Gradual Release of Responsibility

It is important to teach students how to find their own mentor texts because they won't always have teachers to provide them. If you teach students to read like writers and adopt their own mentor texts, you will set them up to be independent and resourceful.

I remember sitting with one of my fourth graders, Kiara, and her parents during a family-teacher conference. She had brought along a copy of *Just Grace* by Charise Mericle Harper. As we started the conference, Kiara opened the book and said she wanted to "write with funky punctuation," as Harper does.

"How come?" I asked, wondering about the reading-writing connection she was making.

"Because it's neat. I don't see those dashes that much in other books," Kiara said. "I want to try that in my own writing."

That weekend, I looked through other just-right-level chapter books and picture books to find more examples of "funky punctuation" for Kiara. Specifically, I wanted to show her more of the ways authors use dashes so she would be clear about when to use a comma versus a dash to set off part of her writing. At the time, we were in a character unit of study in reading workshop. Kiara was not just reading her chapter book and taking notice of things happening to the character, she was also reading like a writer! This is the kind of work I want all students to do. Kids can read like writers if they see their teachers doing this during writing workshop mini-lessons, strategy lessons, and conferences.

But it's not just about punctuation. It's about knowing literature so well that kids can seek books they know from read-aloud or independent reading to use as mentor texts. It's about knowing who the funny authors are when they're writing a humorous piece and who the lyrical authors are when they want to compose something deep. Kids look to beloved books for inspiration. We lay the groundwork, but our students have to do the rest.

Digging into the Texts

Now that you feel more confident about all the ways you can lead small-group lessons in your classroom, let's dig into the meat of this book—the lesson sets. In Chapters 5 and 6, I have included a matrix that summarizes the recommended power craft moves for each picture book featured. You'll notice that some of the moves can be taught with multiple books. I kept the structure and language consistent, recognizing that you might need to teach the same power craft move multiple times to the same small group of writers until they can confidently use the skill on their own. I also realize that you might not be able to purchase all the picture books I've recommended, so the matrix will show you how to maximize those you do have.

The lessons for each book are not exhaustive. I realize there is something that may *wow* you about a book for which I haven't written a lesson. I expect you will find additional things to teach students from each of the twenty picture books featured. Go ahead and teach students how to do those things!

Don't use this book as a manual. I wrote the lessons sets to discourage that. Rather, I hope this book offers many models for teaching craft moves to young writers, but then inspires you to find new mentor texts and learn from them together.

Chapter

5

Fiction Lesson Sets: Ten Texts, Thousands of Possibilities

I believe all students deserve to read mirror books, in which they can see themselves, and window books, in which they can learn about others (Bishop 1990). This means teachers must choose picture books that represent a variety of religions, races, and sexual orientations. Every time I read a picture book for consideration in this book, I looked for two things: power craft moves I could teach to kids and characters and themes that probed the range of human experience. Many of these texts will invite your students to imagine a world or lifestyle different from their own, which may also increase their desire to write with a wider lens.

Figure 5.1 shows the power craft moves supported by ten mentor texts. I have included at least six power craft lessons for each of the featured books. However, keep in mind that these lessons are not the *only* ones you can and should teach. For instance, after I finished developing the lesson sets for *Yard Sale* by Eve Bunting and Lauren Castillo, I thought of more ways I could mine the text for power craft moves. I realized that three triggers had upset the main character, Callie—the bed, the bike, and the "Are you for sale?" incident—during the course of the story. Wouldn't that be a good example of the rule of three, which is when an author draws a reader's attention to and emphasizes something in the text three distinct times? In order to meet my deadline for writing this book, I decided to cut off questions like this. But I hope

	Dialogue	Internal Thinking	Lead/Ending	Punctuation to Create Voice	Repetition	Show, Don't Tell	Specific Details	Structure	Turning Point	Varied Sentence Lengths
Clever Jack Takes the Cake	x		x	x	x	x	x	x		x
Eat, Leo! Eat!	x		x	x	x	x	x	x	x	
Happy Like Soccer	x		x		x	x	x	x		
Henry Holton Takes the Ice	x		x	x		x	x	x	x	
Knuffle Bunny Free	x			x	x		x	x	x	
Last Stop on Market Street	x	x	x	x	x	x	x	x	x	
Mango, Abuela, and Me	x	x	x	x		x	x	x		
Stella Brings the Family	x		x				x	x	x	x
Trouper			x	x	x	x	x	x	x	
Yard Sale	x	x	x	x		x	x	x	x	x

Figure 5.1
Ten fiction mentor texts and their power craft moves

you will continue to ask questions of the books as you get to know them. The possibilities are endless.

Clever Jack Takes the Cake
by Candace Fleming and G. Brian Karas

Publisher's Summary: What would you do if you were invited to the princess's tenth birthday party but didn't have money for a gift? Well, clever Jack decides to bake the princess a cake. Now he just has to get it to the castle in one piece. What could *possibly* go wrong?

Power Craft Move: Dialogue

Name the craft: Dialogue Advances the Story

Why authors do it: Dialogue is one way writers add details to the plot and expand the relationships between characters while also moving the story forward.

How to do this:
- Study at least two places in *Clever Jack Takes the Cake* where Fleming crafts dialogue. Three possibilities:

- Reread pages 8 and 9. Jack is excited about going to the party, but his mom does not having enough money to buy the princess a gift. He decides to bake a cake and give it to the princess.
- Reread page 16. The story would stall if Jack didn't surrender the cake to the troll, but the dialogue reveals the deal Jack makes to get cross the bridge.
- Reread pages 29 and 30. By the time Jack reaches the castle, he has only part of the cake left—the strawberry at the top. The conversation between Jack and the guard makes readers feel deflated because Jack has nothing left to give the princess.
- Share with students how authors use dialogue to advance the plot.
- Invite students to add dialogue where it will help readers understand what's happening between characters *and* advance the story.
  - Have students think about real-life conversations. Students can work with a partner to write the dialogue in the air or act out scenes from their stories.

Power Craft Move:	Ending

Name the craft: Surprise Ending

Why authors do it: Writers want to maintain the interest of their audience throughout their stories. One way writers do this is by crafting an ending readers don't see coming.

How to do this:
- Study pages 28–39.
  - Although the princess is not impressed by the treasures others have bestowed (page 28), she is delighted by Jack's unusual present (page 34). She says, "And an adventure story at that! What a fine gift!" The ending helps us realize the princess is a complex character who is not interested in material possessions. Page 36 shows the princess and Jack sharing stories and cake. A friendship has been formed thanks to the power of story.
  - It is important to show students what the main characters are thinking and feeling. Fleming does this through the dialogue the princess speaks while Karas communicates this further in the final pictures and on the endpapers.

- Invite students to add a twist to the ending of their stories that the reader may not see coming. Encourage them to craft an ending that is believable but will also surprise the reader at the end of their narrative.

Power Craft Move: Lead

Name the craft: Taking a Reader into the Past

Why authors do it: Writers transport their readers back to the past.

How to do this:
- Reread page 7 to your students. This book is considered a modern fairy tale because it doesn't begin with the words "Once upon a time." Instead, Fleming provides clues, such as by writing "long ago."
- Invite students to begin their fairy tale *without* using the words "Once upon a time." Encourage them to play with phrases that include words about time to help their audience understand the story takes place in another period.

Power Craft Move: Punctuation to Create Voice

Name the craft: Hyphenated Words

Why authors do it: Writers join two or more words together to create compound adjectives that are more descriptive and distinctive than ordinary modifiers.

How to do this:
- Study the following examples with students.
  - On page 13, "That same night, Jack stood back to admire his creation—two layers of golden-sweet cake covered in buttery frosting and ringed with ten tiny candles." You could start out by reading the sentence without the hyphenated words and then reread it as it appeared in *Clever Jack*. "Golden-sweet" modifies the word *cake* and helps readers to notice both sweetness and color.
  - On page 14, "Before long, he came to a bloom-speckled meadow." The compound adjective helps readers understand there are flowers growing in the grass, which is why Jack wants to pick a bouquet for the princess.

- On page 16, "Out stepped a wild-haired troll." "Wild-haired" provides readers with a more precise description of what the troll looked like.
- You can also use these examples with students as a form of show, don't tell.
- Invite your students to create adjectives to give their writing voice by combining two or more words with a hyphen.

Power Craft Move: Punctuation to Create Voice

Name the craft: Dashes

Why authors do it: Writers use dashes to emphasize, interrupt, or change a thought in the middle of a sentence. Dashes can be used to set off part of the text so as to draw attention to it. Sometimes dashes are used to create longer or more dramatic pauses before a page turn.

How to do this:
- Study the following places in the text.
  - Page 9: The dashes highlight the few furnishings in the home of Jack and his mother. The dashes make readers linger to think about the ax, the spinning wheel, and the threadbare quilt. The dashes also encourage readers to think about a gift that would be fine enough for the princess.
  - Page 13: The dashes set off the words "in the place of honor." Fleming may have included this phrase inside dashes to draw attention to the strawberry, which is the only part of the cake that remains when Jack arrives at the castle.
  - Pages 20 and 21: Point out that "*Pffft!*" appears inside dashes on both pages. Think aloud about the dramatic pause created by the second set of dashes, which helps readers realize how quickly the candles are burning down.
    - For more sophisticated writers, you could mention that these dashes are setting off onomatopoeia in the text.
- Invite students to create dramatic pauses for their readers by inserting dashes anywhere they wish to draw attention to or encourage readers to linger with a thought or idea.

Power Craft Move: Repetition

Name the craft: Repeated Phrase

Why authors do it: Writers repeat words purposefully when they want to emphasize something in their writing. Writers have to figure out the right words to repeat; otherwise their writing sounds monotonous.

How to do this:
- Study two places in *Clever Jack* where Fleming repeated a phrase.
    - On pages 11, 26, and 29, Fleming refers to the "reddest, juiciest, most succulent strawberry in the land."
        - The emphasis on this strawberry helps readers understand that the strawberry itself can be a gift because it is of such high quality.
    - On page 13, we learn the cake has "two layers of golden-sweet cake covered in buttery frosting and ringed with ten tiny candles. Across the cake's top, walnuts spelled out 'Happy Birthday, Princess.' And in the very center—in the place of honor—sat the succulent strawberry." This list gets repeated four more times in the text.
        - Jack's lament begins on page 16, which explains what's left on the cake after the mishap with the blackbirds. Each subsequent mention of the cake (on pages 18, 21, and 26) follows the same order, but omits the dwindling items after each obstacle on Jack's journey.
- Invite students to reread their narratives. Encourage them to look for a phrase they could repeat several times for emphasis. (It could be in the same sentence or the same paragraph across the text.)

Power Craft Move: Show, Don't Tell

Name the craft: Draw an Image in the Reader's Mind

Why authors do it: One way writers help readers make a movie in their minds is by showing their readers what's happening instead of just telling what's happening. Authors use precise language to show readers what is happening in a scene.

How to do this:
- Study at least two places in *Clever Jack* that help the reader visualize what is happening. Here are some possibilities:
    - Reread page 20, which contains one sentence: "Then he set to work, churning, chopping, blending, baking." This sentence explains all the steps Jack had to take to turn the ingredients he gathered into a cake. Although the cake is central to the

story, baking the cake isn't, which is probably why Fleming devoted one very vivid sentence to explain Jack's process of cake preparation.

- Reread page 27. "Jack looked down at his gift, and for several seconds he was unable to speak." Instead of saying Jack was sad, the author shows that he's rendered speechless. Later on page 27, we see how Jack comes to terms with the spit-out strawberry. He proudly carries it to the castle.
- There are numerous examples of the show, don't tell power craft move in *Clever Jack*. Encourage students to find one if you think it will benefit them to talk about another example before doing this work on their own.
- Invite students to find places in their own writing where they told instead of showing. Encourage them to use more descriptive words to help readers envision what's happening. Remind students to use precise words to describe how characters act, think, talk, or feel.

Power Craft Move:	Specific Details
Name the craft:	Character Details
Why authors do it:	Writers know it's important to include information about what characters are doing in order to make them seem like real people.
How to do this:	• Study some of the details Fleming uses to describe the secondary characters in *Clever Jack Takes the Cake*.

- On page 16, the troll licks his lips, growls, grunts, and slobbers. The descriptions help us understand why Jack is willing to surrender one layer of the cake to the troll.
- On page 28, Fleming describes the princess as sitting "on her velvet throne" and yawning from boredom with the various gifts. These details indicate that the princess is hard to impress because she seems to have everything.
- Encourage students to look for places where they can embed details about characters to help readers understand them.

Power Craft Move:	Specific Details
Name the craft:	Setting Details

Why authors do it: Writers give readers a sense of place through descriptions about the time period, weather, location, and other events.

How to do this:
- Study several places in *Clever Jack Takes the Cake* where the author embeds setting details.
  - On page 18, Fleming helps us envision the woods. She writes, "The road grew narrower. The trees grew thicker. The light grew dimmer. Soon it was so dark that Jack couldn't see the cake in front of his face." Rich setting details prepare readers for the spooky scene that's about to take place.
  - On page 21, Fleming brings us out of the woods, "As it did, the road widened, the trees thinned, and the bright sunlight shone once more." Some readers might feel a sense of relief when Jack is back in the light of day again.
  - On page 26, reread the sentences that take readers to the castle: "Across the drawbridge . . . . Through the fortress walls . . . ." Describing the castle precisely allows readers to know this is a traditional fairy tale castle.
  - Explain that employing a variety of setting details helps readers envision the story without pictures. (This is especially important for intermediate-grade students who may not be illustrating their writing.)
- Invite students to include setting details throughout their narrative.

Power Craft Move: Structure

Name the craft: Beginning-Middle-End

Why authors do it: Stories have distinct parts. Characters and the setting are usually introduced at the beginning of stories. Readers find out what happens to the characters in the middle. By the end, characters usually change in some way.

How to do this:
- Show students the three distinct parts of *Clever Jack Takes the Cake*.
  - The beginning (pages 6–13) takes place in and around Jack's home. We meet Jack and his mom.
  - The middle (pages 14–27) focuses on Jack's walk from his cottage to the princess's castle. We meet a cast of characters along the way.

- The end (pages 28–35) shares how Jack's humble gift could make the princess ill. We listen as he recounts his journey to the castle and witness the princess's delight with Jack's adventure story gift.
- Talk to students about how the parts of the story flow from one to the next. Discuss how setting provides transitions from one part of the story to another.
- Invite students to craft or revise their stories so they have a clear beginning, middle, and end.
  - Students might need to tell the story using their fingers (e.g., first, second, next, then, and finally) if they can't yet grasp the concept of beginning-middle-end. After students write in the air in small-group sessions, encourage them to type or write on paper independently.

Power Craft Move:	Structure
Name the craft:	Movement of Time
Why authors do it:	One of a writer's jobs is to keep the story moving along in a way that helps readers understand time is passing.
How to do this:	• Study the way Fleming uses phrases to help the reader transition.

- Study the way Fleming uses phrases to help the reader transition.
  - On page 7, "One summer morning long ago . . ."
  - On page 10, "And that same morning . . ."
  - On page 13, "That same night . . ."
  - On page 14, "Early the next morning . . ."
  - On pages 16, 18, and 22, "Before long . . ."
  - On page 31, "Now . . ."
  - On page 35, "Then . . ."
- Invite students to move readers through time by including short phrases that transition from scene to scene in their writing.

Power Craft Move:	Varied Sentence Lengths
Name the craft:	Creating Rhythm and Emphasis in Writing
Why authors do it:	Varying the lengths of sentences adds life to writing and helps to guide readers. For example, authors use short sentences and punctuation to encourage readers to pause, stop, and think, whereas they use longer sentences to encourage quicker movement through the text.

How to do this:
- Study at least two places in *Clever Jack* where Fleming varied the lengths of sentences. Some possibilities:
  - Reread page 11. The first two sentences are short: subject, verb, and direct objects. The third sentence is long, with several commas and two sets of ellipsis points. Fleming may have wanted readers to think about what Jack was gathering. The longer sentence makes readers feel as if they're on the hunt, desperately searching for the most perfect strawberry in the land.
  - Reread page 18. Most of the sentences are longer and can be read quickly on this page. However, once Jack arrives at the forest, we are commanded to pause with two short sentences: "No birds chirped here. No squirrels chittered." Fleming might have wanted readers to slow down, feel the eeriness of the woods, and hear the silence.
  - Reread page 31. Point out the following short sentences: "Jack gulped. He blushed. He shuffled his feet." The first two are simple sentences, just a subject and a verb, but the third is a little longer. All three are relatively short compared to those on the rest of the page. Fleming may have written these short sentences to make readers pause. Jack had to think fast, but by drawing attention to what his throat, face, and feet were doing, Fleming encourages us to slow down and think.
- Invite students to vary the sentence lengths in their drafts. Encourage them to craft longer sentences when they want their reader to move right along and shorter sentences when they'd like their reader to focus more on the words contained in the short sentences.

Eat, Leo! Eat! by Caroline Adderson and Josée Bisaillon

Publisher's Summary: Leo wants no part of sitting down with his family to eat Nonna's big, *delizioso* lunch every Sunday. "I'm not hungry," he insists. Not hungry? Hmm. Clever Nonna gets an idea. She'll use a story to lure Leo to her table. She uses the pasta (called *stelline,* or little stars) in her soup as the basis of a story about a boy who journeys to his grandmother's house at night. It works; Leo eats the soup. But on the following Sunday, Leo again doesn't want to eat. So Nonna expands her story, this time adding some *chiancaredde* (paving stones), the name of the pasta she's serving that day, to create a path for her character to follow. Now Leo is hooked, so much so that he begins to badger Nonna every Sunday to reveal more pasta-based details of the story. And week by week, as Leo's relatives crowd around listening to Nonna and teasing Leo to get him to *mangia* (eat), he slowly comes to realize just how happy he is to have a place at this table. In this heartwarming picture book, award-winning author Caroline Adderson beautifully captures the love and tenderness Leo feels from his grandmother and the rest of his close-knit family through lively, true-to-life dialogue. The playful, detailed artwork by Josée Bisaillon helps bring all of the characters to life. This book offers a framework for lessons exploring the heritage, customs, and relationships of families. The unique story-within-a-story concept, along with the idea that Nonna's tale is being told cumulatively, could easily launch a storytelling assignment for young writers. Additionally, the section on pasta and the list of Italian vocabulary words make a great introduction to foreign cultures through food and language.

Power Craft Move:	Dialogue
Name the craft:	Code Switching
Why authors do it:	Dialogue enables readers to experience the events through the language of characters. Writers can use code switching, which is the practice of alternating between two languages in their writing, to make the dialogue sound authentic.
How to do this:	<ul><li>Point out the list of Italian words, pronunciations, and definitions on page 2. Then, study two types of code-switching Adderson employs in *Eat, Leo! Eat!*<ul><li>Examples of words or expressions defined in context, as well as on page 2, for readers:<ul><li>Page 7: "Not hungry for *stelline*? Not hungry for little stars?" Nonna translates the word *stelline* in the second sentence.</li><li>Page 17: "*Occhi di lupo*. Wolf eyes." Readers don't have to flip back to page 2 to find out the meaning of *occhi di lupo* because the translation follows the Italian words.</li></ul></li></ul></li></ul>

- Page 25: "And here's the *creste di gallo,* the rooster's comb." Readers understand what *creste di gallo* means because the comma is followed by the definition of the word. It's defined by Nonna, as she speaks to Leo.
  - Undefined in context (must use translation page):
    - Page 7: "Nonna ladles out the *zuppa.*" Readers must reference page 2 to learn that *zuppa* means soup.
    - Page 12: "*Chiancaredde.* Now *mangia,* Leo." If readers don't recall that *chiancaredde* was defined as paving stones on the previous page, they'll need to refer to the translation page. *Mangia,* which means eat, is used throughout the text. If readers didn't tie the title of the book together with the word *mangia,* they could look it up on page 2.
- Ask students which kind of code switching was easiest for them understand as a reader. Ask them which one felt like less of an interruption while reading *Eat, Leo! Eat!* Both kinds of code switching have their benefits because the person speaking in students' stories might not translate the words as Adderson did. (This is a good time to point out that authors might switch words to make their writing easier for readers. Adderson often defined the words or expressions in context, rather than making readers unfamiliar with Italian look back for the definition.)
- Invite students to add dialogue that alternates between two languages to parts of their stories. Dialogue that employs code switching needs to help readers understand what's happening among characters while also advancing the story.
- Students might try out both types of code switching—defining in context and making use of a translation list—in their writing. From there, they can pick the one they think will work best for their audience.

Power Craft Move: Ending

Name the craft: Accomplishments/Discovery

Why authors do it: Writers create satisfying endings. One way they do this is to show readers how the main character has changed for the better by the end of the story.

How to do this:
- Review pages 26–31 with students.
  - Study the pictures on pages 26–30. Ask students, "What's happening in these pictures?"
    - If necessary, draw attention to Leo helping Nonna make the farfalle on page 26. Point out everyone gathered around the table on page 27. Remind students of the story on pages 28 and 29.
  - Note the story's ending on page 30 (i.e., butterflies surround the boy and Nonna as they hug at the end of Nonna's story), which mirrors the meal they're eating (on page 31). Draw attention to Leo's ending the story on page 31. Note that Leo wishes everyone else a "Buon appetito!" on page 31. By the end of the book, Leo has changed. He learned how to enjoy family dinners.
  - Invite students to try the accomplishments ending that will show their readers how their main character has changed for the better by the end of their piece.
    - Ask students: "How does your character change?" and "How can you show your readers what the main character has accomplished at the end of your story?"

Power Craft Move: Lead

Name the craft: Introducing the Characters Through a Splash of Dialogue

Why authors do it: Writers use this technique to help explain the relationships between characters, create vivid descriptions of the setting, and advance the plot.

How to do this:
- Ask students to close their eyes as you reread pages 4–6 of *Eat, Leo! Eat!* Things you could point out:
  - Adderson introduces the members of the family and shows readers where they are (Nonna's house) and when they are gathered (on a Sunday afternoon). There's a splash of dialogue in the opening pages of the story, which helps set up the problem: Leo doesn't want to join the rest of the family for lunch.
    - This type of lead is helpful for teaching students that too much dialogue in the beginning of the story can get messy.

By using Adderson's lead, you can show your students how to introduce readers to the characters in an interesting way.

- Invite students to craft a lead that will help readers meet the characters in their stories. Note that Adderson didn't name every person by name, nor did she give away too much information about what they'd be eating. Instead, Bisaillon's illustrations of lots of feet on pages 4 and 5 help us understand there are many people in Nonna's house at lunchtime. Have students sketch what the first scene looks like and then have them craft just the right words to introduce their characters to their readers. Encourage them to add a splash of dialogue, as Adderson did, somewhere in the first few paragraphs to bring their characters to life.

Power Craft Move: Punctuation to Create Voice

Name the craft: Dashes

Why authors do it: Writers use dashes to emphasize, interrupt, or change a thought in the middle of a sentence. Dashes can be used to set off part of the text so as to draw attention to it. Sometimes dashes are used to create longer or more dramatic pauses before a page turn.

How to do this:
- Study the following places in the text.
  - Page 5: There are two dashes on this page. The first dash interrupts the sentence to tell readers who is gathered at Nonna's house for Sunday lunch. The second dash serves a different function, which is to get us to pause before turning the page, which is where we find Leo hiding under a table because he doesn't want to eat lunch.
  - Page 22: Here's a dash that forces readers to pause. It's as if Adderson wanted to slow readers down since something out of the ordinary happened the following Sunday afternoon. The dash changes our mind-set and alerts us to the surprise, which is that Leo was the first person at the table.
- Invite students to create dramatic pauses for their readers by inserting dashes anywhere they wish to emphasize part of the text. Anytime writers want their readers to linger with a thought or idea, they can employ a dash to create a longer pause.

| **Power Craft Move:** | Specific Details |

Name the craft: Sensory Details

Why authors do it: Strong writing appeals to the five senses. Writers can create concrete images so that their writing comes to life.

How to do this:
- Study two places in the text where Adderson included sensory details.
    - Page 26 allows readers to **feel** the crank on the pasta maker and the dough that is being unrolled, cut, and pinched into farfalle.
    - Page 29 enables readers to **see** the starlight in the sky and the way the wolves moved, **hear** the rooster crowing, and **feel** the sun's warmth.
    - Pages 29–30 help readers **see** thousands of colorful butterflies.
- Explain that Adderson uses words such as *crowing, pinches, prowled, unroll,* and *warm* to help readers see, hear, or feel something.
- Invite students to read through their drafts to search for places where they can add sensory details to activate their readers' five senses.
    - Tip: You might caution your young writers not to overdo it with sensory details. For instance, "The boy opened the heavy door," works better than "The young boy pulled the heavy, blue door open with his sweaty palm." Encourage students to include only the details that will help a reader envision the story without overwhelming their senses.

| **Power Craft Move:** | Structure |

Name the craft: Movement of Time

Why authors do it: One of a writer's jobs is to keep the story moving along in a way that helps readers understand that time is passing. Writers craft sentences that move their readers from scene to scene in their writing.

How to do this:
- Study the way Adderson uses phrases to help the reader transition through time from scene to scene in the story.
    - On page 5, "On Sunday afternoons . . ."
    - On page 10, "The next Sunday afternoon . . ."

- On pages 15 and 18, "The next Sunday afternoon . . . ." These are the third and fourth Sundays readers find Leo refusing to eat.
- On page 23, "The next Sunday afternoon—surprise!" This marks the fifth week, but the first time Leo voluntarily comes to the table.
- On page 26, "And the next Sunday . . . ." We see a change in Leo since he arrived early at Nonna's house to help her prepare the meal (and to try to get the story out of her a bit earlier).
- Note that the author uses "next" to show succession and notes the day of the week, "Sunday," every time a week advances.
- Invite students to move readers through time by including short phrases, which will help readers to transition from scene to scene in their writing.

Power Craft Move:	Turning Point
Name the craft:	Pivot Point
Why authors do it:	Pivot points are those defining moments when something of great significance happens to the main character. A turning point moves the story forward when the main character changes in a significant way.
How to do this:	• Study the turning point in *Eat, Leo! Eat!*

- Study the turning point in *Eat, Leo! Eat!*
  - Reread pages 22–23. The turning point takes place when Leo is the first person at the table. But he doesn't want to eat. Instead, Leo wants to hear the story. He knows the story and lunch go together, so he calls the rest of the family to lunch. After a month, Leo seems like he's ready to change. Readers see him show up to the table and hear him call the rest of the family in for lunch. These are important moments that show how Leo is changing over time.
- Invite students to craft or revise the turning point in their stories, using the following questions to guide them:
  - Does the main character undergo any kind of change in order to overcome the story's conflict?
  - Does the main character have a new understanding that changes his or her perspective of everything else that's happened?
  - Does the main character discover a new situation for the first time?

Happy Like Soccer by Maribeth Boelts and Lauren Castillo

Publisher's Summary:

Nothing makes Sierra happy like soccer. Her shoes have flames as she spins the ball down the spread-out sea of grass. But nothing makes her sad like soccer, too, because the restaurant where her auntie works is busy on game days and she can't take time off to watch Sierra play. On game days, Sierra's auntie helps her get ready and tells her, "Play hard and have fun." And Sierra does, but she can't help wishing she had someone there to root for her by name, and not just by the number on her uniform. With honesty and rare subtlety, author Maribeth Boelts and illustrator Lauren Castillo portray an endearing character in a moving, uplifting story that touches on the divides children navigate every day, reminding us that everyone needs someone to cheer them on from the sidelines.

Power Craft Move: Dialogue

Name the craft: Dialogue Advances the Story

Why authors do it: Dialogue is one way writers add details to the plot and expand the relationships between characters while also moving the story forward.

How to do this:
- Study at least two places in *Happy Like Soccer* where Boelts crafts dialogue. Two possibilities:
  - Reread page 12. Boelts tells us about Auntie's conversation with her boss. Perhaps it was summarized because it was a long conversation. Show students the spoken interaction between Sierra and Auntie. Hypothesize that their conversation was written out so the author could show readers that Sierra's auntie cares about her, even if she cannot be at every game.
  - Reread page 27: Boelts summarizes the story of how Sierra got the game rescheduled and moved to their neighborhood. Auntie and Sierra exchange words and a hug. The author may have written out this conversation to show a deep love and caring between the two.
  - Discuss the way authors summarize unimportant conversations by telling us what happened. This will help students understand that authors use dialogue to move stories forward purposefully.

- Invite students to add dialogue to places in their stories that will help readers understand the relationship between characters *and* will move the story forward.
  - Have students star a few places where their stories might benefit from having some dialogue.
  - Encourage students to craft one section of dialogue before they head back to their seats.

Power Craft Move: Ending

Name the craft: Circular Ending

Why authors do it: A circular ending is one where the action of the story returns to the themes mentioned at the beginning. Essentially, the story ends where it began.

How to do this:
- Review excerpts from the text so you can note how the ending is circular.
  - Page 9: Reread the beginning of *Happy Like Soccer* where everyone on Sierra's team has someone cheering for them in the stands except for her. Remind students that Sierra worked with Coach Marco to bring the final game to the field in her neighborhood.
  - Examine the ending on pages 28–29. Point out how we see and hear Sierra's auntie and the people from her neighborhood cheering for her *by name*. Show how the action comes back to a soccer field. Note there are similar words on pages 9 and 29.
- Invite students to try a circular ending. One way to do this is to have students think back to the beginning of the story. They might ask themselves, "Can I have my story end in the same place, with the same characters, with just a bit changing?"

Power Craft Move: Lead

Name the craft: Compare/Contrast Lead

Why authors do it: A good story needs a lead that hooks the reader. One way writers draw their readers into their stories is by comparing and contrasting emotions, which shows the complexity and oppositional pull of characters' thoughts. This creates an immediate conflict, which sparks interest in what will happen.

How to do this: • Reread the first two pages of *Happy Like Soccer*.
  • Initially, Sierra talks about how happy soccer makes her. Once readers turn the page, they discover the reasons soccer also makes her sad.
  • The idea of being *picked* for a new team with "these shiny girls" creates a positive mood. But on the next page, there's a sense of sadness and disappointment that follows our main character.
  • Readers are drawn into world of the story by comparing and contrasting the two fields, as well as the two reasons soccer makes Sierra feel happy and sad.
• Invite students to craft a compare/contrast lead.
  • Encourage students who need a push to think about their main character's life. Are there any differences or contrasts (i.e., what's on the surface versus what lies beneath)? They can do some jotting in their writer's notebook, which will help them figure out some aspect of the main character's life or situation they can compare and contrast.

Power Craft Move: Repetition

Name the craft: Power of Three

Why authors do it: Writers often repeat a word, phrase, or line in order to have a desired effect. One technique is known as the power of three, a type of repetition done three distinct times in order to draw attention to something.

How to do this: • Study two places in *Happy Like Soccer* where Boelts uses the power of three.
  • On page 17: "I swallow, sure that the rescheduled last game will be on a Saturday, sure it will be outside of the city, sure my auntie's boss won't do two favors in a row."
    • Boelts used the word *sure* three times in one sentence. She may have done this to build an emotional connection between the reader and Sierra's strong emotions when she knows her auntie will probably miss the final rescheduled game of the season.

- On page 22: "I take a breath and tell him I'm sorry for it being late, and then I say my idea fast and all run-on, that maybe the game could be on a Monday, and maybe it could be at the lot by my apartment, and then maybe my auntie could come?"
  - Think aloud about how Sierra's saying "maybe" reflects her tentative, timid mood. Reading the word *maybe* three times helps us realize Sierra doesn't want to inconvenience everyone else even though she wants her aunt to attend her final soccer game.
- Invite students to revise at least one place in their writing using the power of three. Encourage students to reread their writing and then revise a part of their text, using the power of three, on a large sticky note.

Power Craft Move: Show, Don't Tell

Name the craft: Draw an Image in the Reader's Mind

Why authors do it: One way writers help readers make a movie in their minds is by using precise language to show their readers what's happening instead of just telling.

How to do this:
- Study at least two places in *Happy Like Soccer* that draw an image in the reader's mind. Here are three possibilities:
  - On page 5: "I smile, but when she hugs me good-bye, I know she can feel me low around the edges." The word *low* is a richer way to say Sierra was sad.
  - On page 10: "I bite my lip without meaning to and tell him no." When Sierra bites her lip, readers sense her hesitation. Readers might think she wants to ask for a favor, but she's afraid to, so she says no. Boelts shows how Sierra looked uneasy rather than telling us she was.
  - Page 29: "And I hear my name because they know *me*, not just my number. And above the rest, I hear my auntie's strong voice cheering me on." Readers might think Sierra is happy because the final game was rescheduled in her neighborhood. Boelts doesn't tell us she is happy, but readers sense it since she finally hears people cheering for her by name.

- Invite students to elaborate on important parts of their story, especially the parts that contribute to the deeper meaning. They might provide details, insert internal thinking, or include small actions to show readers what's happening with the characters.

Power Craft Move:	Specific Details

Name the craft: Sensory Details

Why authors do it: Strong writing appeals to the five senses. Writers can create concrete images so that their writing comes to life.

How to do this:
- Study at least two places in the text where Boelts included sensory details. Here are some possibilities:
  - Page 5 allows readers to **feel** the way Sierra's auntie helps her get ready when they read: "Early every game day, my auntie looks me over good—brushes my hair, rubs my legs with lotion."
  - Page 16 enables readers to **hear, see,** and **feel** the way the weather ruins the soccer game since Boelts writes: "Fat rain-drops plopping. Then thunder starts its show, and in the distance, lightning."
  - Page 25 lets readers **hear** what Sierra hears when we read: "City sounds are all around, mixed with my auntie's steady breathing, and my own self noisy with what I want to happen."
- Boelts uses words like *brushes, plopping,* and *rubs* to help readers feel. Similarly, she helps readers hear thunder, city noises, and Auntie's breathing with the words she chooses. Readers can envision the lightning in the sky.
- Invite students to read through their draft to search for places where they can add sensory details to activate their readers' five senses.
  - Caution your writers not to overdo it with sensory details. For instance, "The girl sat down abruptly" works better than "The short girl with curly hair sat down in the red chair abruptly." Encourage students to include only the details that will help readers envision the story without overwhelming their senses.

Power Craft Move:	Structure

Name the craft: Movement of Time and Place

Why authors do it: Authors need to move readers from place to place and through time in a story that has multiple scenes and settings. Some authors move readers through time and place in a very subtle way.

How to do this:
- Study movement through time and place at the beginning, in the middle, and at the end of *Happy Like Soccer*. The number of examples you give your students will depend on the amount of experience they have with crafting these kinds of transitions independently.
  - The beginning of the story:
    - Page 6: We leave Sierra's neighborhood when she gets into the car with other girls. The text says, "We weave past the empty lot and through my neighborhood and outside the city, where the buses don't run." This part of the text shows that it takes a while for Sierra to get to the soccer field in the suburbs.
    - Page 11: After the game, we take a similar trip: "[W]e ride back home, into the city, through my neighborhood, past the empty lot, and right to the restaurant, where my auntie brings me chicken and noodles." This is the reverse trip, perhaps so we can understand how far Sierra has to travel back home.
  - The middle of the story:
    - Page 12: Boelts writes, "Then on Friday, my auntie tells me that her boss has heard me talking . . . ." The words *then* and *Friday* show the passage of time.
    - Page 14: Sierra and her auntie take multiple buses to the soccer field. This shows how difficult it is for them to get to the game.
    - Page 16: The game gets canceled.
    - Page 18: Coach Marco gives Sierra and her auntie a ride home.
    - Page 21: Sierra has an idea. Boelts writes, "My auntie is asleep, so I tiptoe to the kitchen." This sets us up for the phone call Sierra makes to Coach Marco.
    - Page 25: Sierra has to wait for an answer from Coach Marco, which seems agonizing. We can feel how long she must wait

by the way Boelts writes, "It is a long time until morning." This made me feel as tense as Sierra must have felt.
- The end of the story:
  - Page 26: We don't know how much time has passed because Boelts simply starts this page with the word *later*.
  - Page 27: "I run home, skipping the stairs two at a time." As readers, we can feel Sierra's sense of excitement as she races home to tell her auntie the final game will be held in their neighborhood.
  - Page 28: We know the story is coming to a close since this page begins with the words, "[A]t the last game . . . ."
- Remind students they can make references to time (minutes, hours, days), meals, seasons, and time of day to help readers understand the passage of time in their stories.
- Invite students to read through their narratives, keeping sequence and seamless transitions in mind. Their revision goal could be to revise their story so it flows as smoothly as *Happy Like Soccer*.
  - Remind students they can do this by using words that will signal their reader to how time is moving and to where characters are going.

Henry Holton Takes the Ice by Sandra Bradley and Sara Palacios

Publisher's Summary: Henry Holton's whole family is mad about hockey. Everyone, that is, except Henry. When he holds a hockey stick, Henry becomes a menace to the game—and an embarrassment to his sports-minded family. It's not until he sees his first ice-dancing performance that Henry realizes there's something he can do on the ice that *doesn't* involve boarding and body checking. Henry is ready to hang up his gear and try on some figure skates, but first he has to convince his hockey-obsessed family to let him follow his own path.

Power Craft Move: Dialogue

Name the craft: Dialogue Advances the Story

Why authors do it: Dialogue is one way writers add details to the plot and expand the relationships between characters while also moving the story forward.

How to do this: • Study three places in *Henry Holton Takes the Ice* where Bradley crafted dialogue that advances the plot. Some possibilities:

- Reread pages 13 and 14. The dialogue on page 13 tells the reader, and Henry's mom, what he wants. Readers might hope Henry's father will see his point of view, but on page 14, it's clear that Henry's father won't be persuaded easily. Readers can sense Henry's frustration when his father and sister shut down his request on page 14.

- Reread pages 20 and 21. Make note of the kinder tone between Grandma and Henry. Readers get a sense she might help Henry get what he wants since she used to be a figure skater. Grandma's hockey-infused soliloquy on page 21 may have been written to help Henry realize she felt strongly about playing hockey the first time she picked up a stick. When Henry asks her if she still has her skates, we get a sense the answer is going to move the story forward.

- Reread page 27 and study the illustration. Perhaps Henry initiates the conversation with his father when he gets off the ice in order to make sure his dad noticed the magical experience he had on the ice. Dad's acknowledgment makes it clear that he is happy Henry found something he loves on the ice. Draw students' attention to the smile on Henry's face and the grin on Dad's face, as well as the way Dad is patting Henry's head. These illustrations match the tone of the dialogue on this page.

• Talk with students about the power of dialogue. Help them understand that authors use dialogue to advance their stories by thickening the plot and allowing readers to experience what the characters are actually saying.

• Invite students to add dialogue to places in their stories that will help readers understand what's happening between characters *and* will advance the story.

- Have students think about real-life conversations. Students can work with a partner to write in the air or act out a scene from their stories. Then, ask students to write that dialogue for a given section in a way that will advance their stories before they head back to their independent writing focus spots.

Power Craft Move:	Ending

Name the craft:	Accomplishments/Discovery Ending

Why authors do it:	Characters change or grow in stories. One way writers can illustrate this is by having the characters accomplish something.

How to do this:	• Reread pages 29–31. Study the pictures as well as the words in order to glean additional meaning.

      • Point out the way Henry keeps working and trying to balance until he glides across the ice. This is a great accomplishment, which is reflected in the final page spread of the book. Note that his immediate family and Grandma are watching his first lesson. When Henry finally glides across the ice on one foot, his family applauds. Point out the line where Grandma hollers, "*Henry Holton, you beauty*! I knew you'd make one *fine ice dancer*!" (Note: A variation of this line appears on page 6, when Grandma originally says Henry would make "one *fine hockey player*.") Ask students: What's different between the responses of Henry's immediate family and his Grandma?

   • Invite students to show the way in which their characters changed at the end of their stories by making note of their accomplishments.

Power Craft Move:	Lead

Name the craft:	Meeting the Characters

Why authors do it:	Writers bring readers into the world of the story by introducing the main and secondary characters immediately.

How to do this:	• Reread pages 2–5 of *Henry Holton Takes the Ice*.

   • Things you could point out:

      • The first page of the story—words and pictures—helps readers understand that Henry's family lives and breathes ice hockey. Readers are immediately brought into their hockey-loving family by the end of page 3. On page 3, we learn that Henry's mom drives a Zamboni at work and their dog, named after hockey great Wayne Gretzky, wears hockey gear. By page 5, readers see a young Henry teething on hockey pucks and getting a pair of baby skates tied onto his tiny feet. It is clear this family is obsessed with ice hockey.

- The pictures on pages 2 and 3 support the text in the first paragraph. Readers see trophies and framed ice hockey photos on the walls of the Holton home. There are hockey photos of everyone *except* Henry.

- Invite students to bring their audience into the world of their stories by introducing the main character (and possibly the secondary characters) from the very first paragraph.

  - Encourage students to go beyond listing names and physical descriptions of the people in their stories. Have them include important details, like Bradley does by writing about Grandma being MVP of the Silver Skates League and dressing the dog in hockey gear, to make the characters come alive. Remind students to include just enough about the characters in the lead of their story so they draw in their audience in without overwhelming them with too many character details.

Power Craft Move:	Punctuation to Create Voice
Name the craft:	Ellipsis Points
Why authors do it:	Writers punctuate their texts to help readers read with expression. Punctuation like ellipsis points makes the reader's voice trail off when reading dialogue aloud.
How to do this:	• Study two places in the text where the authors use ellipsis points.

- Study two places in the text where the authors use ellipsis points.
  - Reread page 11. Notice how the ellipsis points cause Mom's thoughts to trail off before you turn the page. We know Mom is part of the hockey family and the ellipses may reflect the hesitation she's feeling about taking Henry to the ice dancing club's extravaganza.
  - Reread page 14. The ellipsis points come at the end of the last thing Henry says to try to convince his father (and sister) that ice dancing isn't just for girls. Henry's thought is complete but his voice drifts off, making the reader feel his despondence; no one seems to be listening to what he's saying.
  - For more sophisticated writers, you might note the sentence-terminating period before the ellipsis points in both examples.

Talk with students about why Bradley includes a sentence-terminating period. Is it because the sentence is complete, but the thought continues?

- Invite students to craft some writing with ellipsis points or to revise by inserting ellipsis points. Suggest including ellipsis points anytime students want to show some hesitation in a character's voice or want to have a thought trail off.

Power Craft Move:	Show, Don't Tell
Name the craft:	Draw an Image in the Reader's Mind
Why authors do it:	One way writers help readers make a movie in their minds is by using precise language to show their readers what's happening, instead of just telling.
How to do this:	• Study at least two places in *Henry Holton Takes the Ice* that help the reader envision what is happening. Here are some possibilities:

- Reread page 8. Readers learn that Henry is the strongest skater in Holton history, but he refuses to hold a hockey stick. As readers, we twist, turn, weave, sway, and shimmy with Henry. Precise verbs help us understand how Henry moved around the rink.
- Reread page 12. We see how Henry views the skaters as they move across the ice in time with the music. He compares them to "brightly colored kites, swirling and twirling in the wind." We get a sense of how magical Henry finds ice dancing as he watches from the bleachers with his "mouth open, heart pounding."
- Reread page 24. We learn that Henry feels *just right* on the ice even though it is different from his usual skating. We can feel him wobble because he wears too-big skates, and we can stand straight with him as he skates. The writing on this page is concise and helps readers feel as though they're on the ice with Henry the first time he steps out in skates with picks.
- Reread page 29. We're right there as Henry tries and tries to "dash down the ice, spin like a top, and finish with one foot high in the air." The writing is vivid, which means readers can almost picture it before Henry is able to do it.

- Invite students to find places in their writing where they tell the reader what is happening. Encourage students to draw an image in their readers' minds by elaborating. Students might provide details, add dialogue, or include small actions to show readers what's happening with their characters.

Power Craft Move: Specific Details

Name the craft: Character Details

Why authors do it: Writers know it's important to include information about what characters are doing in order to make them seem like real people to their readers.

How to do this:
- Study Henry at three points in *Henry Holton Takes the Ice*.
  - On pages 16 and 17, we see Henry holding a sign that requests skates with picks. We learn he benched himself for weeks, refusing to put on his Junior Pro skates. This shows readers Henry isn't afraid to stand up for what he believes in. On page 17, he tells his mom that he needs to dance rather than skate. Henry's quiet protest and his easygoing manner of disagreeing with his mom show that he is a respectful person.
  - On pages 18 and 19, readers can look inside Henry's bedroom and see posters of animals, a basketball hoop, and robot figurines. The illustration shows a hockey stick and a Junior Pro skate in the garbage. Henry's grandmother enters in an attempt to get him back on the ice. He tells her, "I'm not a hockey player. I wasn't made for boarding and body checking." Readers learn that Henry has a strong sense of self.
  - On page 29, we notice Henry trying very hard to slide across the ice, spin, and then "finish with one foot high in the air." This helps readers learn that Henry is willing to persevere because he wants to ice skate.
- Invite students to include pertinent character details in their writing by thinking about aspects of their main character. Encourage them to look for places where they can embed details about their characters that will help readers get to know the kind of people they are.

Power Craft Move:	Specific Details

Name the craft: Rule of Three

Why authors do it: Writers create a rhythmic quality to their writing by writing in sets of three—three actions, a sequence of three things, three characters, and so on—which draws a reader's attention to that part of the text.

How to do this:
- Study two places in *Henry Holton Takes the Ice* where Bradley uses the rule of three to bring out things that were happening to or with the main character.
  - On page 6: "He swished, swooshed, and swaggered."
    - Bradley uses three verbs to show the way Henry glides across the ice with ease.
  - On page 8: "He swayed and shuffled and shimmied."
    - Here are three more verbs that show what Henry looks like as he strides across the ice without his stick.
  - The number three is mentioned several times in the story. On page 22, we learn Henry brings three pairs of wool socks so his feet will fit in the skates. On page 26, the man who runs the rink drags Henry off of the ice after he whistles three times.
    - You might ask students, "Why not four? What's so magical about the number three?"
  - On page 25, Henry ignores three things: his sister, everything around him, and the bell that signals the end of the free skate. Point out that Bradley uses the word *ignore* three times on this page.
- Invite students to find at least one place in their writing where they can emphasize what's happening with the character by employing the rule of three. Encourage students to reread their writing and then revise a part of their text, using the rule of three, on a large sticky note.

Power Craft Move:	Structure

Name the craft: Movement of Time

Why authors do it: One of a writer's jobs is to keep the story moving along in a way that helps readers understand that time is passing. Writers craft sentences that move their readers from scene to scene in their writing.

How to do this: • Study the way Bradley uses phrases to help the reader transition through time from scene to scene in the story.
  • On page 8, "By the time Henry was seven . . ."
  • On page 11, "And then, one day . . ."
  • On page 16, "And for weeks . . ."
  • On page 19, "Then, one day . . ."
  • On page 22, "That night . . ."
  • On page 28, "The next day" and "When they got to the rink"
  • Note: Bradley used phrases to signal age, time of day, or the amount of time to move readers through time.
• Invite students to move readers through time by including short phrases that will help them transition from scene to scene.

| **Power Craft Move:** | Turning Point |

Name the craft: Pivot Point

Why authors do it: Pivot points are those defining moments when something of great significance happens to the main character. A turning point often moves the story forward because the main character changes in a significant way.

How to do this: • Study the turning point in *The Henry Holton Takes the Ice*.
  • Reread pages 22–25. The turning point takes place when Henry goes to the rink and puts on his grandmother's old ice skates. In the background, we see his grandmother's anticipation and joy as he prepares to go on the ice. On pages 24 and 25, we notice that Henry is joyfully skating across the ice, ignoring everything except for the music and his feet. Talk about the importance of this scene as Henry's transformation from a non-pick ice-skater and protester to an ice dancer (it's a pretty decisive change!). Discuss the way Palacios's illustrations convey Henry's happiness and inattention to everything around him except for what he's doing.
• Invite students whose stories feel flat to use a story mountain to locate the turning point. Remind students that the turning point should be at the height of the story mountain. It could be an emotional or action-filled scene, a revelation, or a defining moment. Encourage students to think as authors do: building tension for

their characters as they climb the mountain, increasing the challenges until they are able to change, and then finally reaching a resolution on the way down the mountain.

- If students have not created a story mountain in the past, you can show them how the author of *Henry Holton Takes the Ice* creates more of a rising slope more than a straight-up-and-down story mountain. Bradley and Palacios shape their story like an arc: instead of a mountain with the peak in the middle, their turning point occurs near the end of the book.

Knuffle Bunny Free: An Unexpected Diversion by Mo Willems

Publisher's Summary: Trixie and her family are off on a fantastic trip to visit her grandparents—all the way to Holland! But does Knuffle Bunny have different travel plans?

An emotional tour de force, *Knuffle Bunny Free* concludes one of the most beloved picture-book series in recent memory, with pitch-perfect text and art, photos from around the world, and a stunning foldout spread, culminating in a hilarious and moving surprise that no child or parent will be able to resist.

Power Craft Move: Dialogue

Name the craft: Speech Bubbles

Why authors do it: Writers add details to their writing by having their characters speak. Speech bubbles allow characters' voices to be heard in a story while moving the plotline forward.

How to do this:
- Study at least two places in *Knuffle Bunny Free* where Willems uses speech bubbles. Two possibilities:
  - Reread pages 15 and 16: This is the first place in the text where we encounter a speech bubble. Talk about the way the speech bubble reinforces the austerity of the situation. Also, the speech bubble highlights just one word, the name of the place where the plane flew, within a sentence.
  - Reread pages 35–41: This part of the text contains more speech bubbles. Start by thinking aloud about why Willems

might have included more dialogue in this part of the text rather than at the beginning of the book. Wonder aloud about how hearing the characters' voices moves the story forward.

- You could make mention of the different types of speech bubbles: jagged purple bubbles for the baby and smooth pink and blue bubbles for Trixie and the adults.
- Tip: Only point this out if you are meeting with writers who won't spend inordinate amounts of time color-coding speech bubbles.

- Talk about the sparse use of speech bubbles throughout the text. Giving a nod toward a *less is more* mind-set might prevent speech bubbles from popping up all over your students' next drafts because this technique should be employed as a way to purposefully advance one's narrative.
- Invite students to insert speech bubbles (such as into the picture part of their paper) so they can give their characters a voice while moving their story forward. Emerging writers might include empty speech bubbles in the sketch (above their writing) to note a place where the characters are conversing.

| **Power Craft Move:** | Punctuation to Create Voice |

Name the craft: Cadence

Why authors do it: Writers craft their words intentionally to help their readers know how to read them. Cadence is the way that writers stress or emphasize points in their writing. The rhythm of writing urges readers forward and keeps them engaged.

How to do this:
- Study at least two places in *Knuffle Bunny Free* where Willems uses cadence. Be sure to stress the way commas are used in each of the sentences to help readers modulate their voices:
  - On page 5, "One day, not so long ago, Trixie took a big trip with her family." Reread this sentence aloud twice. After the first reading, students listen to you modulate your voice when you read the first sentence of the book. The insertion of the phrase *not so long ago* gives readers an idea of when the story happened, without being overly specific. This provides readers with the context instead of just jumping to telling the reader that Trixie took a big trip with her family.

- On pages 36 and 37, "Right there, on that very plane, Trixie noticed something. . . ." Reread the text from this page aloud, purposefully modulating your voice. Ask students if they noticed the way your voice changed when you read the phrase *on that very plane* or how your voice trailed off after the word *something*. The commas and ellipsis points signal cadence. Also, think aloud about how the rhythm of the writing pushed you forward as a reader.
- On pages 43 and 44, "And that is how, a few weeks later, Trixie received her very first letter!" Read this aloud so your students hear how your voice modulates. The rhythm of this sentence is similar to the construct of the first sentence in the book. The final sentence provides readers with a time frame followed by an action (Trixie receiving her first letter).
- Invite students to use punctuation and short phrases to create voice in their drafts.
  - You might teach students about the idea of copy change. Essentially, students can use the same pattern or sentence structure as Willems does while changing the rest of the words so it fits their writing.
    - Teach students to thank the author, in this case Willems, in an acknowledgment section at the end of their published writing for the copy change.

Power Craft Move:	Punctuation to Create Voice

Name the craft: Parentheses

Why authors do it: Sometimes authors add parentheses to clarify something for readers or to convey a conversational tone.

How to do this:
- Study two places in the text where Willems includes information in parentheses as a way of being friendlier with readers.
  - Reread pages 7–9. The words on that page spread are part of one long sentence. Talk about how many things happened before the family boarded the plane, which might be why Willems includes the word *finally* in parentheses. The insertion of the word helps readers feel strongly about what's happening.

- Reread pages 22–24. Point out how the parentheses on page 22 are almost like a secret the author is sharing with the reader. Show the illustration of Oma and Opa tiptoeing into the store to buy something for Trixie. Trixie doesn't know they're sneaking off, but as readers, we know they are doing so because of the illustration and clues in the parentheses. Mention that there are two sentences in two separate sets of parentheses. Think aloud about why Willems chose to put them in two sets of parentheses, as opposed to one.
  - There are parentheses on page 24, but they seem to be there more for clarification and less for enhancing the writer's voice.
- It is important to show students how few parenthetical references there are in the text so as to make sure they don't overuse them (just as Willems doesn't overuse them in his book).
- Invite students to insert parentheses sparingly into their writing. Remind them they can include information in parentheses anytime they want to get more conversational with their readers—just as Willems does in *Knuffle Bunny Free*.

Power Craft Move:	Punctuation to Create Voice
Name the craft:	Ellipsis Points
Why authors do it:	Writers punctuate their texts to help readers read with expression or to slow down.

How to do this:

- Study at least two places in the text where Willems uses ellipsis points.
  - Reread pages 9–11. Notice how the ellipsis points cause one's voice to trail off before you turn the page. Willems continues the sentence on the following page because Trixie's arrival takes a lot of time. Perhaps Willems wants us to linger over the words on the preceding page. Or, he may continue the text on the following page because he wants to have a large illustration accompany Trixie's arrival at Oma and Opa's house.
  - Reread page 25. The ellipsis points continue on to the next page to suggest the way we drift off into a dream (slowly).

The ellipsis points open up to text that includes some of the same words (but in a different tense) as in the phrase "She was dreaming." Theorize that Willems wants readers to linger before turning the page to find out what Trixie dreamed about that night.

- Reread page 36. Ellipsis points are positioned in a way that encourages us to linger with a complete thought a little longer. Mention how ellipses make us consider that something unexpected is about to happen. In this case it's pretty shocking, considering what happened up until this point in the story. So, perhaps that's why Willems includes the ellipses—because he wants to make readers pause and think a bit before going on.
- For sophisticated writers: Note that there is a sentence-terminating period before the ellipsis points in two of the three examples. Talk with students about why Willems includes it. Is it because the sentence is complete, but the thought continues? Is the sentence-terminating period omitted in one example because the sentence continues on the next page?
- Invite students to craft some writing with ellipsis points or to revise by inserting ellipsis points. Suggest they include ellipsis points anytime they want to create an extended pause, have a thought trail off, or omit something that comes after a complete sentence.

Power Craft Move:	Specific Details
Name the craft:	Precise Information
Why authors do it:	Writers know it's important to include precise information about what characters are doing in order to make their writing come alive for their readers.
How to do this:	• Study two places in the text where Willems includes precise information to help readers understand what is happening in the story.

- Reread pages 21 and 22. Willems could have said the whole week is filled with fun things, but he provides readers with precise information about the things the family does together.

Further, the illustrations enhance the text by showing what the family is doing.

- Reread pages 31 and 32. Again, Willems might have said Trixie has a great day after she dreams of finding Knuffle Bunny. Instead, he provides precise information, with photos that match the text, to show how wonderful Trixie's day is. Remind readers that specific details help readers know what their characters are going through, so they seem like real people who could jump off the page.

- Invite students to add precise information to their character descriptions. Encourage students to look for places where they might have summarized and nudge them to include specific details that will help readers understand what their characters are doing.

Power Craft Move:	Specific Details
Name the craft:	Rule of Three
Why authors do it:	A way to create a rhythmic quality to writing by using sets of three: three actions, a sequence of three things, three characters, and so on. Anything done three distinct times tends to draw a reader's attention to and emphasize a section of text.
How to do this:	• Study at least two places in *Knuffle Bunny Free* where Willems uses the rule of three.

  - Reread page 9: Show this series of three actions with three accompanying illustrations. Willems may have chosen to show three actions to lend balance to what is happening on the plane.
  - Reread page 24: Think aloud about how three actions by the Funny-Bunny-Wunny-Doll Extreme show readers just enough about the doll's features to make it amusing. You might say, "Who wouldn't love a doll like that?" Answer your question with a response that lets your students know that it wasn't enough to amuse Trixie since Knuffle Bunny couldn't easily be replaced.
  - Reread pages 25–30: The clause "she dreamed" reinforces the fact that Trixie is able to fall asleep despite thinking she wouldn't. All Trixie's thoughts about Knuffle Bunny, while she

sleeps, are positive. She dreams of the changes in Knuffle Bunny's life rather than focusing on how upset she is.

- Reread page 40: Start by noticing that each person says the same word: "Really?" Hypothesize that each person asks for a different reason. For instance, the baby's mother probably asks because she is shocked that Trixie would give her stuffed animal to a child she doesn't know.

- Invite students to repeat a word or phrase to create rhythm in their writing. Ask them to find a place or two in the text that will make that section stand out to their readers.

Power Craft Move:	Structure
Name the craft:	Beginning-Middle-End
Why authors do it:	Stories have distinct parts. Characters and the setting are usually introduced at the beginning of stories. Readers find out what happens to the characters in the middle. By the end, characters usually change in some way.
How to do this:	• Show students the three distinct parts of *Knuffle Bunny Free*.

  - The beginning of the story goes from pages 5–11. The story begins at Trixie's home. It quickly moves through the airport, onto the airplane, and to the train station. The sequence of events is quick. We meet Trixie and her parents and find out where Trixie is going (Oma and Opa's house).
  - The middle of the story goes from pages 12–33. We witness Trixie's reaction to Knuffle Bunny's disappearance. We get to see how Trixie copes without Knuffle Bunny. We also get to see her grow as a character by learning she can thrive without Knuffle Bunny.
  - The end of the story goes from pages 34–44. The story wraps up when Trixie and her parents get back on the plane. She finds Knuffle Bunny but gives him away to a crying baby to make him feel better.
    - Pages 45–48 include Daddy's note to Trixie. Although this could be considered part of the end of the story, I suggest leaving this out because it feels more like an epilogue to me.

- Talk to students about how the parts of the story flow from one to the next. Discuss the change that takes place for Trixie as she goes from missing Knuffle Bunny to coming to terms with all the children Knuffle Bunny might cheer up. This enables her to enjoy the end of her trip to Holland without Knuffle Bunny.
- Invite students to craft or revise their stories so they each have a clear beginning, middle, and end.
  - Students might need to tell the story across their fingers (e.g., first, second, next, then, and finally) if beginning-middle-end is a tough concept for them. Later, encourage them to write on paper after they leave the small-group session.

Power Craft Move:	Turning Point
Name the craft:	Pivot Point
Why authors do it:	Pivot points are those defining moments when something of great significance happens to the main character or when she or he has an epiphany. A turning point often moves the story forward because the main character changes in a significant way.
How to do this:	• Study the turning point in *Knuffle Bunny Free*.

- Study the turning point in *Knuffle Bunny Free*.
  - Reread pages 25–30. The turning point takes place while Trixie is dreaming. Mention that Trixie is unsure if she can sleep another night without Knuffle Bunny, but she feels better after her night of imagining all the wonderful things Knuffle Bunny is doing without her. Point out that she has a great day *after* her dream.
  - Some students might think finding Knuffle Bunny on the plane is the turning point in the story. If so, you may want to ask them some of the following questions to help them identify the turning point both in *Knuffle Bunny Free* and in their writing.
    - How does the main character (Trixie) take a big step to overcome the story conflict (in this case, losing Knuffle Bunny)?
    - How does the main character imagine new possibilities?
    - What new perspective or new understanding does the main character reach?

- What realization does the main character come to that affects the rest of the story?
- Invite students to craft or revise the turning point in their stories. Ask students some of the previous questions to help them think about and define it. Students have to know what their turning point will be before they can write that part of their narrative with precision.

Last Stop on Market Street by Matt de la Peña and Christian Robinson

Publisher's Summary: Every Sunday after church, CJ and his grandma ride the bus across town. But today, CJ wonders why they don't own a car like his friend Colby. Why doesn't he have an iPod like the boys on the bus? How come they always have to get off in the dirty part of town? Each question is met with an encouraging answer from his grandma, who helps him see the beauty—and fun—in their routine and the world around them.

Power Craft Move: Dialogue

Name the craft: Dialogue Advances the Story

Why authors do it: Dialogue is one way writers add details to the plot and expand the relationships between characters while also moving the story forward.

How to do this:
- Study at least two places in *Last Stop on Market Street* where de la Peña crafts dialogue. Two possibilities:
  - Reread pages 14 and 15. CJ is watching the world go by outside the bus and is questioning why his life is different than other kids' lives. Nana is content with their life and tries to reassure CJ that his life is better off because he goes somewhere after church.
  - Reread pages 18 and 19. Three people are speaking on these pages: CJ, Nana, and the blind man. Nana points out to CJ that he doesn't need the iPod he sees the other boys using when he has a guitar player on the bus playing live music. CJ takes a cue from the blind man and Nana to close his eyes so he can savor the music being played.

- Talk with students about the power of dialogue. This will help students understand that authors use dialogue to advance their stories by thickening the plot, allowing readers to experience what is happening in the story through the characters' voices.
- Invite students to add dialogue to places in their stories to help readers understand what's happening between characters *and* advance the story.
  - Have students think about real-life conversations. They can work with partners to write in the air or act out a scene from their stories. Then, ask students to write their dialogue for a given section in a way that will move their stories forward before they head back to their writing spots.

Power Craft Move:	Internal Thinking
Name the craft:	Creating Characters' Emotional Lives
Why authors do it:	Writers use a variety of details to show what's happening to the characters in their stories. Internal dialogue is one method writers use to help readers understand a character's thinking.
How to do this:	• Study two places in *Last Stop on Market Street* where de la Peña includes CJ's internal thoughts.

  - Reread page 26. The sentence that begins with "He wondered" shows readers what CJ is thinking as he observes the rainbow over the soup kitchen. Readers realize that he wouldn't be thinking about the beauty present before him if Nana hadn't encouraged him to look for it. Knowing what CJ is thinking on this page helps readers understand how he is changing as a character.
  - Reread pages 28–30. When Nana pats CJ on the head (page 30), he is surprised because he expected her to laugh at him for changing his mind about coming to the soup kitchen. This is like real life because we cannot always predict how others are going to react to something we say.
- Invite students to include internal thinking in their narratives.
  - Creating an internal-external time line is one way to get students in the habit of including internal thinking into their writing. If students have already created a time line with

actions, then they just need to add thought bubbles to capture the character's thinking associated with each action.

- Another way is to have students provide details about characters' relationships. Students can create a web or diagram showing what the main character feels about, needs from, thinks about, or wants from each of the secondary characters.

Power Craft Move: Ending

Name the craft: Lesson Learned with Dialogue

Why authors do it: Characters change or grow in stories. One way writers can illustrate the change is by having characters learn a lesson.

How to do this:
- Reread pages 25–31. Study the pictures on the page spreads as well as the spoken words between CJ and his Nana in order to glean additional meaning.
  - CJ is initially unhappy about going to the soup kitchen to see the people Nana talked about (see page 15). On the walk to the soup kitchen, CJ questions why it's so dirty in this part of the city, which can mean he's still unhappy about where he is. Nana helps CJ understand that sometimes being surrounded by dirt can help a person search deeper for beauty. After Nana speaks to him, CJ observes a rainbow over the soup kitchen. Once he sees familiar faces inside the soup kitchen, CJ declares that he is happy they came to serve others. CJ stands alongside Nana smiling as he serves food (page 31). This shows him being helpful. CJ's admission that he's glad he came to the soup kitchen shows he has changed his mind about the way Nana has him spend his time after church. He has found the beauty in the neighborhood (pages 26 and 27) and the familiar faces. As a result, the reader can infer that he realizes it's not what material possessions he has, but finding joy in the ordinary and taking care of others that matters.
  - Remind students they reveal a lot with carefully chosen dialogue at the end of their writing. Sometimes, as in the case of the few but powerful spoken lines between CJ and Nana, a little bit of dialogue goes a long way toward conveying how a character learns a lesson to readers.

- Invite students to show the way in which their main character changes by the end of their story. One way they might want to show this is through the use of dialogue like that between Nana and CJ.

Power Craft Move:	Lead

Name the craft: Appeal to the Senses

Why authors do it: Authors appeal to readers' senses when they want to make them feel as if they are in the settings described in the book.

How to do this:
- Reread pages 4 and 5 of *Last Stop on Market Street*.
- Things you could point out:
  - Readers are drawn into the story because the author starts by describing a specific location (outside church). De la Peña provides rich details that wake up the senses, such as what the outdoors smell like (freedom and rain) and feel like (wet from the rain falling on CJ's clothes and face).
  - Also, readers get a sense of place by examining the illustrations that show people holding umbrellas on a city street.
  - It will always improve a description if writers use more than one sense in their writing. Two to three senses will be enough to help readers take in the world of the story. Sight, smell, and touch are excellent senses to encourage students to use when crafting leads with sensory details.
    - Tip: Help students understand that using all five senses would be overwhelming to readers! We want students to craft sincere writing, not writing that sounds forced or phony.
- Invite students to craft a lead using sensory details.
  - Encourage students to use their senses to ground their characters in the setting and build the worlds of the stories with their words. Have students write down what the setting looks like, smells like, and so on. Encourage students to include just enough about the setting in the leads of their stories so they draw their readers in without overwhelming them with sensory description.
  - Some students might want to employ onomatopoeia. Rather than letting them just throw in a sound word or two,

encourage them to incorporate sound only if it has something to do with the rest of their story.

Power Craft Move:	Punctuation to Create Voice

Name the craft: Hyphenated Words

Why authors do it: Writers join two or more words together to create compound adjectives that are more descriptive and distinctive than ordinary modifiers.

How to do this:
- Study the following examples with students.
  - On page 24, "Crumbling sidewalks and broken-down doors, graffiti-tagged windows and boarded-up stores." Start out by reading the sentence without the hyphenated words, and then reread it as it is written in *Last Stop on Market Street*. "Broken-down" modifies the word *doors*, "graffiti-tagged" refers to the windows, and "boarded-up" reshapes the word *stores*. These compound adjectives provide readers with a vivid picture of what the area looks like.
    - You can also use this example as a form of show, don't tell.
  - On page 27, the author writes that CJ "looked all around them again, at the bus rounding the corner out of sight and the broken streetlamps still lit up bright and the stray-cat shadows moving across the wall." They're not shadows of cars or people; they're the cats that are roaming the street, which provide a clearer picture for readers of what the neighborhood looks like.
- Invite your students to create compound adjectives to give their writing voice.

Power Craft Move:	Repetition

Name the craft: Repeated Phrase

Why authors do it: Writers repeat words purposefully when they want to emphasize something in their writing. They have to figure out the right words to repeat; otherwise their writing sounds monotonous.

How to do this:
- Study two places in *Last Stop on Market Street* where de la Peña repeats a phrase.

- On pages 12, 17, and 30, de la Peña refers to Nana's "deep laugh."
  - The deep laugh characterizes Nana as a happy person. This allows us to understand what is important to her (what she finds funny and what she takes seriously) when she doesn't let out her deep laugh at the end of the story.
- On page 14: "The bus lurched forward and stopped, lurched forward and stopped."
  - The repeated phrase emphasizes an action. Readers can almost feel the way the bus is moving through the city streets.
- Invite students to reread their narratives. Encourage them to look for a phrase they could repeat for emphasis several times. (It could be in the same sentence or the same paragraph or across the text.)

Power Craft Move:	Show, Don't Tell
Name the craft:	Draw an Image in the Reader's Mind
Why authors do it:	One way writers help readers make a movie in their minds is by using precise language to show their readers what's happening instead of just telling.
How to do this:	

- Study at least two places in *Last Stop on Market Street* that show, rather than tell, the reader what is happening. Here are some possibilities:
  - Reread page 5. De la Peña shows readers how the air smells, both symbolically and physically. He does this by using a simile to compare the air to freedom and then he says it smells like rain. He also shows how the raindrops look on CJ's shirt and his face. Instead of saying it is raining, de la Peña shows readers exactly what it looks like and smells like when CJ exits the church.
  - Reread page 10. Emphasize the way words like *creaked,* *sighed,* and *sagged* (all verbs) show readers, rather than tell them, how the bus sounded and moved as it approached the bus stop. You could change the sentences to something more generic when explaining this to students (e.g., "The bus stopped as the door swung open") and then think aloud about

how de la Peña's sentences help readers feel like they're actually there alongside CJ and Nana at the bus stop.

- Reread the first sentence on page 14. The repetition of the phrase "lurched forward and stopped" shows the way the bus moved rather than just saying, "The bus came to a stop." Talk about the strong words de la Peña chose to show, rather than tell, readers how the bus moved through the city streets.

- Invite students to find a place in their writing where they tell readers what is happening and encourage them to revise by showing what's happening. Ask students to use actions, thoughts, dialogue, or feelings to help readers understand their characters. Empower sophisticated writers to elaborate in a way that reflects the big meaning or theme of their narratives.

Power Craft Move:	Specific Details

Name the craft: Character Details

Why authors do it: Writers provide details to make characters seem like real people to their readers.

How to do this:
- Study Nana at several points in *The Last Stop on Market Street*.
  - On page 13, Nana is the kind of person who greets everyone on the bus with a smile and a "good afternoon." Nana makes sure CJ also greets people on the bus. This shows Nana is the kind of person who has good manners. Nana's desire to sit close to the front of the bus might show her age in that she doesn't want to walk too far back.
  - On page 14, reread the sentence "Nana hummed as she knit." Ask students, "What does this sentence reveal about Nana?" Elicit their ideas and then talk about some of the things this sentence made you think or feel about Nana. Talk about why de la Peña chose to include this character detail in the story.
  - On pages 16 and 17, we see Nana squeezing the blind man's hand and laughing her "deep laugh" after he compliments her on her perfume. This is a way Nana sets other people at ease and connects with them.
  - When readers look at the sum of these details about Nana (and others in the story) it is easier to understand how she's

able to teach CJ about embracing what he has and finding the beauty in the ordinary. Nana leads by example.
- Invite students to include pertinent details in their writing by thinking about all aspects of their characters.

Power Craft Move:	Specific Details

Name the craft: Setting Details

Why authors do it: Writers give readers a sense of place by including vivid descriptions of the settings. Details can focus on the time period, weather, location, and more.

How to do this:
- Study several places in *The Last Stop on Market Street* where setting details are embedded.
  - On page 8, mention where they are (bus stop) and what is happening (rain is pooling on the flowers and pattering on the windshields).
  - On page 24, start by rereading the sentence about what CJ sees after he disembarks from the bus: "Crumbling sidewalks and broken-down doors, graffiti-tagged windows and boarded up stores." Talk about how de la Peña creates such a powerful image with his words.
  - On pages 26 and 27, make note of the variety of setting details, such as weather (rainbow) and social conditions (soup kitchen and broken street lamps).
  - Explain that employing a variety of setting details helps readers envision the story without pictures. (This is especially important for upper elementary students who are most likely not illustrating their writing.)
- Invite students to include a balance of setting details throughout their narrative. Encourage them to use precise language to describe the setting to create a sense of place.

Power Craft Move:	Structure

Name the craft: Heart of the Story

Why authors do it: Writers ask themselves, "What is the heart of my story?" Then they reveal this focus bit by bit rather than summarizing it.

How to do this:
- Study the heart of the story alongside students.
  - Start with a quick picture walk of pages 12–23 to reorient students with the heart of the story. (This is from the moment CJ and Nana board the bus to the time Mr. Dennis calls their stop.)
    - Tip: You might wish to prepare a time line of the events on pages 12–23 to show students as you demonstrate.
  - Mention that the heart of the story begins on page 12 with specific dialogue ("What's that I see?") and an action (a coin being pulled from CJ's ear).
  - We're able to visualize the things that happen on the bus in a step-by-step fashion: where CJ and Nana sit, how they greet others, how the bus moves, the conversation they have, the interaction with the man with the spotted dog, observing the boys with the iPod, listening to the guitar player, giving the coin to the musician, and disembarking the bus. These things happen gradually, across pages.
  - Through a variety of details—action, dialogue, setting, thoughts, and interactions—the author reveals the heart of the story across the pages.
- Invite students to identify the heart of their stories. One way students can unfold their stories slowly is to create a time line just for the heart of them.

Step Into a Classroom: Unfolding the Heart of the Story with *Last Stop on Market Street*

I had the pleasure of spending time in Brandy Hurley's first/second-grade classroom when I was working on this book. In early February 2015, I met with Brad, Charlotte, and another of their classmates so I could help them see that realistic fiction writers craft stories that have problems rather than easy solutions or pat story lines. In an extended lesson, I helped them think of adventures that might happen to their characters. Later that month, Brad and Charlotte had started stories about their characters for the fiction series they were writing, but the texts weren't well structured. Brandy asked me to teach them more about structure.

Brad and Charlotte came to the lesson with their writing folders. I asked them to remove their in-process stories and turn to the most important part. Then I asked them if they had summarized that part or unfolded it bit by bit. They looked. They found what I expected them to find: a summary of the most important part of their stories.

Brandy had already read *Last Stop on Market Street* before my visit. I took Brad and Charlotte on a quick picture walk of pages 12–23 to reorient them to the heart of the story, which takes place while Nana and CJ are on the bus. I mentioned that the heart of the story took up eleven pages of de la Peña's book. I noted that the author had included action, dialogue, setting, thoughts, and interactions through the heart of the story, unfolding the story bit by bit. I also showed the students a time line I had created to represent this process and then gave them paper to create their own time lines for the heart of their stories (see Figure 5.2).

Figure 5.2
Brad and Charlotte refer to *Last Stop on Market Street* as they create time lines to structure their own fictional writing.

Power Craft Move:	Turning Point
Name the craft:	Pivot Point
Why authors do it:	Pivot points are the defining moments when something of great significance happens to the main character or when she or he has an epiphany. A turning point often moves the story forward because the main character changes.

How to do this:
- Study the turning point in *The Last Stop on Market Street*.
  - Reread pages 20–22. The turning point takes place while CJ's eyes are closed and he's listening to the guitar player on the bus. Make note of the previous scene where CJ laments not having an iPod. On page 22, CJ opens his eyes and gives a coin to the guitar player, which shows his gratitude for helping him notice the music in his everyday life. CJ's perspective starts to change, as if he has new eyes for the world around him.
- Invite students whose stories feel flat to create a story mountain to locate the turning point. Remind students that the climax should be at the height of the story. It could be an emotional scene, a character's epiphany, or a defining moment. Students should make sure there is rising action that builds to the peak of the story (i.e., the turning point), which will be the most prominent part (of the story).
  - If students have not created a story mountain in the past, show them how by creating a time line for the sequence of events in *Last Stop on Market Street*.

Mango, Abuela, and Me by Meg Medina and Angela Dominguez

Publisher's Summary: Mia's *abuela* has left her sunny house with parrots and palm trees to live with Mia and her parents in the city. The night she arrives, Mia tries to share her favorite book with Abuela before they go to sleep and discovers that Abuela can't read the words inside. So while they cook, Mia helps Abuela learn English ("Dough. *Masa*"), and Mia learns some Spanish too, but it's still hard for Abuela to learn the words she needs to tell Mia all her stories. Then Mia sees a parrot in the pet-shop window and has the *perfecto* idea for how to help them all communicate a little better. An endearing tale from an award-winning duo that speaks loud and clear about learning new things and the love that bonds family members.

Power Craft Move: Dialogue

Name the craft: Code Switching

Why authors do it: Writers use dialogue to let readers hear the exchange of language between characters while moving the story forward. Writers can use code switching, which is the practice of alternating between two languages in their writing, to make the dialogue sound real.

How to do this:
- There are a couple types of code-switching Medina employs in *Mango, Abuela, and Me.* This craft lesson focuses on the words or expressions defined in context:
  - Page 23: "'*Buenas tardes,* Mango,' Abuela says, opening his cage door when I get home from school." Mia says "good afternoon" in Spanish on the next line, which helps readers understand *buenas tardes* means "good afternoon." On the third line, Mango repeats *buenas tardes,* which reinforces that the greeting is being repeated.
  - Page 31: "'*Hasta mañana,* Abuela,' I say. Abuela kisses me. 'Good night, Mia.' '*Hasta mañana.* Good night,' Mango calls." Readers understand that *hasta mañana* is something one might say to another person at the end of the day. (It means "see you tomorrow.") Mango's line makes it clear that he is contributing to the conversation by using a little Spanish and a little English to wish Mia and Abuela good night.
  - Point out how defining words in context on the same page benefits non-Spanish-speaking readers. Note that there are times the words aren't defined in context, which makes comprehending the text harder for a non–Spanish speaker.
- Invite students to add dialogue that alternates between two languages to parts of their stories. The dialogue that employs code switching needs to help readers understand what's happening between characters while advancing the story.

Power Craft Move: Internal Thinking

Name the craft: Creating Characters' Emotional Lives

Why authors do it: Writers use a variety of details to show what's happening to the characters in their story. Internal dialogue is one method that writers use to help readers understand a character's thinking.

How to do this:
- Study two places in *Mango, Abuela, and Me* where Medina includes Mia's internal thoughts.
  - Reread page 3. We learn at the end of the page that Mia feels uncomfortable with Abuela, whom she doesn't know well. She

tells us, "I still feel shy when I meet this far-away grand-mother." This helps readers understand that Mia is timid because of the language barrier and because she has not spent much time with Abuela.

- Reread pages 9 and 10. Mia admits her Spanish isn't good enough to tell Abuela how she is feeling. Readers can infer this makes Mia feel sad because she wants to have a relationship with her grandmother. On page 10, Mia explains that she wants to hear Abuela's stories about her family and where she comes from, but her grandmother doesn't know enough English to share.
  - Mia's internal thoughts set up the problem in the story. Her internal thinking allows readers to understand why she's upset so they can root for her as she solves the language-barrier problem.
- Invite students to include internal thinking in their narratives to show what's happening on the inside to their characters.
  - If your students are familiar with story arcs, which map the structure of their stories, you can encourage them to create an internal story arc to track the main character's internal changes. Once they've plotted the main character's internal changes, they can weave in some of the character's internal thoughts at various points in their narrative.

Power Craft Move:	Ending

Name the craft: Wraparound

Why authors do it: One way writers create satisfying endings is by ending the text with a whisper of the lead.

How to do this:
- Reread pages 28–31.
  - Study the pictures on pages 28 and 29 with your students. Then look back to pages 4 and 5. Ask students, "Does something about the ending remind you of the beginning of the book?"
    - If students don't notice the similarities, point out that Mia and Abuela are in their beds in the bedroom, but there are differences. Ask students, "What's the same and what's different?"
  - Draw attention to the text on page 28 that notes they're both lying in their beds, but this time their "mouths are full of

things to say." That's different than page 4, where Abuela doesn't have the English words to say anything to Mia.

- Make note of the conversation between Mia and Abuela on page 7. Abuela shows Mia things and says only two words in Spanish. On page 31, Abuela kisses her granddaughter and wishes her a good night in English.

- Invite students to try a wraparound ending that harkens back to the lead of their story.
  - Encourage students to look back at their leads, paying close attention to the things their characters say, do, or think.

Power Craft Move:	Lead

Name the craft: Character Snapshot

Why authors do it: A writer can bring readers into the world of the story by providing them with revealing information about the characters in a story.

How to do this:
- Reread pages 3 and 4 of *Mango, Abuela, and Me.* Things to point out:
  - Readers learn Abuela lived far away from her son, Papi, in a warm place surrounded by water. Readers can infer Abuela recently lost her husband because the text says, "Her old place was too much for just one."
  - We learn Mia is shy when she meets her "far-away grandmother" who only speaks Spanish.
- Invite students to craft a lead that provides a snapshot of the main characters in their stories.
  - Encourage students to think deeply about their characters. Have them jot notes about where their characters come from, what makes them happy or sad, and what they're thinking. Ask students to use these notes to create a snapshot of their characters. Remind students that the snapshots must reveal something about the characters to their readers.

Power Craft Move:	Punctuation to Create Voice

Name the craft: Dashes

Why authors do it: Writers use dashes to emphasize, interrupt, or change a thought in the middle of a sentence. Dashes can be used to set off part of the text so as to draw attention to it.

How to do this: • Study the following places in the text.
- Page 7: "A feather—*una pluma*—from a wild parrot that roosted in her mango trees and snapshot—*una fotographia*—of a young man with Papi's smile." There are two sets of dashes on this page. Each set of dashes interrupts the sentence to offset a Spanish word.
- Page 22: "Soon we are playing *Oye y Di*—Hear and Say—all around the house." The dashes in this sentence allow Medina to translate from Spanish into English. They act like commas by introducing new information into the sentence, thereby enhancing it.
- If you have students who are writing in two languages, you can encourage them to use dashes, as Medina does, to translate words for their reader.
- Invite students to create pauses by inserting dashes anywhere they wish to emphasize part of the text. Remind students that anytime they want their readers to linger with a thought or idea they can employ a dash to create a longer pause.

Power Craft Move: Punctuation to Create Voice

Name the craft: Hyphenated Words

Why authors do it: Writers join two or more words together to create compound adjectives that are more descriptive and distinctive than ordinary modifiers.

How to do this: • Study the following examples with students.
- On page 3, "But I still feel shy when I meet this far-away grandmother." Start by reading the sentence without the hyphenated words, and then reread it as it was written in *Mango, Abuela, and Me. Far-away* modifies *grandmother.* This compound adjective helps readers to understand that Mia's Abuela is someone she doesn't know well and probably doesn't see often because she had lived far away.
- On page 19, "Sometimes there are kittens sleeping in the pet-shop window." The pet-shop window isn't pictured in the

illustration, but readers can envision a large glass window filled with kittens sleeping in a variety of nooks.
- On page 20, "And right in the middle is a parrot staring at us with black-bean eyes." The precise description of the parrot's eyes makes the parrot easier to envision.
- Invite your students to create compound adjectives to enhance their writing voice.

Power Craft Move: Punctuation to Create Voice

Name the craft: Vocative Case

Why authors do it: Writers use commas to offset the name of a person or thing that's being addressed in a sentence. A direct address may come at the beginning, middle, or end of a sentence.

How to do this:
- Study the following examples with students.
  - On page 3, "'And too far away for us to help,' Papi adds. 'Abuela belongs with us now, Mia.'" A comma is used to offset Mia's name when Papi is speaking directly to her. The sentence would be complete without Mia's name, but we know exactly to whom Papi is speaking because Mia's name is present.
  - On page 13, "Now Miss Wilson sometimes has to say, 'Please be quiet, girls. Others are working.'" More than one person can be addressed when someone is speaking. In this case, "girls" refers to Mia and her friend Kim.
  - On page 31, "'*Hasta mañana*, Abuela,' I say. Abuela kisses me. 'Good night, Mia.'" Even though there is a dialogue tag in the first sentence, the writer is capturing the real words Mia says to Abuela. Because she directly addresses Abuela in the first sentence, a comma precedes the name. In the second sentence, we understand that Abuela is responding to Mia because she says good night and then says Mia's name. A comma separates Mia's name so the reader can hear the real words Abuela says to her.
- Go to Grammar Monster for more information on the vocative case, http://www.grammar-monster.com/lessons/commas_with_vocative_case.htm.

- Invite your students to include the name of people or things that are being directly addressed in their writing by inserting a comma (or commas if the name comes in the middle of the sentence).

| Power Craft Move: | Show, Don't Tell |

Name the craft: Draw an Image in the Reader's Mind

Why authors do it: One way writers help readers make a movie in their minds is by using precise language to show their readers what's happening instead of just telling.

How to do this:
- Study two places in *Mango, Abuela, and Me* that help the reader visualize what is happening. Here are some possibilities:
  - On page 7, "Snuggled in my pajamas, I smell flowers in her hair, sugar and cinnamon baked into her skin." Readers can share Mia's feelings as she prepares to go to sleep for the first night beside Abuela.
  - On page 20, "I press my nose to the glass, thinking of the red feather Abuela gave me." This sentence explains how Mia looks in at the parrot. It also reveals how she is remembering back to something Abuela shows her earlier in the book. The sentence Medina includes is richer than simply saying "Mia stared at the parrot and thought about something Abuela showed her before."
  - On page 23, "During the day, Abuela teaches him how to give beaky kisses and to bob his head when she sings 'Los Pollitos' to him." Instead of saying "Abuela taught him how to give kisses and move to the music," the author shows what kind of kisses and how she teaches him to move to the music.
  - There are additional examples of show, don't tell, in *Mango, Abuela, and Me.* If students need additional practice, encourage them to find another spot in the text to discuss the power of this move before having them use it in their own writing.
- Invite students to find places in their writing where they tell the reader what is happening. Once students have located at least one place, encourage them to use more descriptive words to help

readers envision what's happening. Remind students to use precise words to describe how their characters act, think, talk, or feel.

Power Craft Move:	Specific Details
Name the craft:	Setting Details
Why authors do it:	Writers give readers a sense of place by including descriptions of where and when their stories occur. Setting could be a description of a place, time period, weather, location, or time of day.
How to do this:	

- Study at least two places in *Mango, Abuela, and Me* where setting details are embedded.
  - On page 4, Medina helps readers understand how Abuela is communicating something to Mia right before bedtime. "Then, just before we turn out the light, she pulls out two things tucked inside the satin pocket of her suitcase." The description makes whatever is about to be revealed more special.
  - On page 16, Medina makes the family's living room look like a classroom when she writes, "Then I remember the word cards we taped in our classroom to help Kim. So, while Abuela fries our *empanadas,* I put up word cards, too, until everything is covered—even Edmund." Readers who have been in school can envision that Mia has turned her house into a living classroom to help Abuela learn English.
  - On page 19, Medina lets us know the family lives in a city because "Mami and I have to ride the bus downtown to buy more" seeds.
  - On page 28, Medina helps readers envision Abuela and Mia in the same room before bedtime: "[W]hen Abuela and I are lying next to each other in our beds, our mouths are full of things to say."
  - Explain that employing a variety of setting details helps readers envision the story without pictures. (This is especially important for upper elementary students who probably aren't illustrating their writing.)
- Invite students to include a balance of setting details throughout their narrative. Encourage them to use precise language to describe the setting to create a sense of place for their readers.

Power Craft Move:	Structure

Name the craft: Heart of the Story

Why authors do it: Writers ask themselves, "What is the heart of my story?" Then they reveal it little by little rather than summarize.

How to do this:
- Study the heart of the story alongside students.
  - Start with a quick picture walk of pages 18–25 to reorient students with the heart of the story. (This is from the moment Mia and Mami go downtown to buy more hamster food to when Papi discovers Mango's new language skills.)
    - Tip: You might prepare a time line of the events on pages 18–25 to show students as you demonstrate.
  - Mention the heart of the story begins on page 18 when Mia cannot help Abuela practice English because she has to travel to the pet store with her mother.
  - We're able to visualize the things that happen in the pet store and when Mia returns home with Mango in a step-by-step fashion: approaching the pet store, discovering the parrot, declaring her intentions for how the parrot will help Abuela, showing the parrot to Abuela for the first time, naming the parrot Mango, teaching Mango phrases, and practicing new words, and Papi discovering what Mango can do. These things happen gradually, across pages.
  - The author uses a variety of details, including action, dialogue, setting, thoughts, and interactions across pages.
- Invite students to identify the heart of their stories. One way students can unfold their stories is by creating a time line just for the heart of them.

Power Craft Move:	Structure

Name the craft: Movement of Time

Why authors do it: One of a writer's jobs is to keep the story moving along in a way that helps readers understand time is passing. Writers craft sentences that move their readers from scene to scene in their writing.

How to do this:
- Study the way Medina uses phrases to help the reader transition through time from scene to scene in the story.

- On page 3: "She comes to us in winter . . ."
- On page 4: "Then, just before we turn out the light . . ."
- On page 7: "That night . . ."
- On page 9: "The rest of the winter . . ."
- On page 14: "After school the next day . . ."
- On page 19: "But the next day . . ."
- On page 23: "When we bring him home . . ."
- On page 25: "Before long . . . ; Soon . . ."
- Note: Some of the phrases include time of day or seasonal information to help us understand the passage of time. A few of the phrases include transitional words, including *after, but,* and *then.*
- Invite students to move readers through time by including short phrases that will help them to transition from scene to scene in their writing.

Stella Brings the Family by Miriam B. Schiffer and Holly Clifton-Brown

Publisher's Summary: Stella's class is having a Mother's Day celebration, but what's a girl with two daddies to do? It's not that she doesn't have someone who helps her with her homework, or tucks her in at night. Stella has her Papa and Daddy, who take care of her, and a whole gaggle of other loved ones who make her feel special and supported every day. She just doesn't have a *mom* to invite to the party. Fortunately, Stella finds a unique solution to her party problem in this sweet story about love, acceptance, and the true meaning of family.

Power Craft Move: Dialogue

Name the craft: Dialogue Advances the Story

Why authors do it: Dialogue is one way writers add details to the plot and expand the relationships between characters while also moving the story forward.

How to do this:
- Study two places in *Stella Brings the Family* where Schiffer crafts dialogue that advances the plot.
  - Reread pages 14 and 15. The dialogue on page 14 shows one of Stella's friends caring about her, wondering why she isn't

eating. On pages 14 and 15, the exchanges between Stella and her friends capture their curiosity about her two fathers. Stella is confident about her family structure and has answers for all of her friends' questions.

- Reread pages 16–18. The questions Stella's friends pose sound real. We hear more questions from Stella's classmates, along with her explanations. This helps Stella's friend Jonathan realize Stella has lots of special people in her family, so he encourages her to invite them all to the class's Mother's Day celebration. The dialogue on these pages shows readers that families don't just look one way.
- Talk with students about the way authors use dialogue to advance their stories.

- Invite students to add dialogue to their stories that will help readers understand what's happening between characters and advance the story.
  - Have students think about real-life conversations. Students can work with partners and use finger play to work out a scene from their stories and figuratively write in the air. Then, ask each student to write that dialogue for a given section in a way that will move the story forward.

Power Craft Move:	Lead
Name the craft:	Action Lead
Why authors do it:	Writers bring readers into the world of the story by starting with some action.

How to do this:	• Reread pages 8 and 9 of *Stella Brings the Family.*
	• Things you could point out:
	  • We see Stella getting a hug good-bye from her dads on the opening page of the book. Readers can see and feel the love they share.
	  • There are two strong verbs on page 9: *dashed* and *raced.* We can feel Stella's eagerness to move around the classroom quickly to find out what surprise Mrs. Abbott has planned.
	• Invite students to bring readers into the world of their stories by having their main characters engage in actions.
	  • Encourage students to include vivid verbs to bring readers into the story quickly.

Power Craft Move:	Specific Details

Name the craft:	Character Details

Why authors do it: Writers know it's important to include information about what characters are doing in order to make them seem like real people to their readers.

How to do this:
- Study Stella at three points in *Stella Brings the Family*.
  - On pages 12–14, we find Stella unable to focus in art class and soccer. We also learn she is unable to eat. This shows her concern about the situation. Her lack of focus also shows readers how worried she is about the Mother's Day party.
  - On page 19, we see Stella in bed, unsure of whether she should invite her dads and her extended family to the school event. The illustration matches the description of Stella, who is grasping her bunny, with furrowed brows, awake in her bed at night. Readers can sense Stella's hesitation about how to proceed.
  - On pages 20 and 21, we are told the children worked hard to make invitations and decorations and prepare gifts. We learn "Stella worked harder than everyone." This shows Stella's determination to make the party as perfect as possible for her guests.
- Invite students to include pertinent character details in their writing by thinking about aspects of their main character.

Power Craft Move:	Specific Details

Name the craft:	Rule of Three

Why authors do it: Writers create a rhythmic quality by writing in sets of three: three actions, a sequence of three things, three characters, and so on. Anything done three distinct times tends to draw a reader's attention to that part of the text.

How to do this:
- Ask students if they notice how Schiffer communicates Stella's feelings. You can have students study two places in *Stella Brings the Family* where Schiffer uses the rule of three to bring out things that are happening to Stella.

- On pages 12–14, there are three events that show Stella preoccupied and affected by the upcoming Mother's Day celebration in her classroom. Point out that the afternoon of the announcement Stella looks at her clay in art class. The following day Stella is thinking about the party instead of the soccer ball that's traveling toward her head. And all week, Stella has no appetite.
- On pages 15 and 16, there are three questions that bring out Stella's friends' curiosity about how her life functions without a mother:
  - "But who packs your lunch like my mom does for me?"
  - "But who reads you bedtime stories like my mothers do for me?"
  - "But who kisses you when you are hurt?"
- Invite students to find at least one place in their writing where they can emphasize what's happening with their characters by employing the rule of three. Encourage students to reread their writing and then revise a part of their text on a sticky note using the rule of three.

Power Craft Move:	Structure

Name the craft: Beginning-Middle-End

Why authors do it: Stories have distinct parts. Characters and setting are usually introduced at the beginning of stories. Readers find out what happens to the characters in the middle. By the end, characters usually change in some way.

How to do this:
- Show students the three distinct parts of *Stella Brings the Family*.
  - The beginning of the story goes from pages 8–11 and takes place at school. We meet Stella, her dads, her teacher, and her classmates.
  - The middle of the story goes from pages 12–21. Readers sense Stella's conflicted emotions about who to bring to her class's Mother's Day celebration.
  - The end of the story spans pages 22–30. The story closes when Stella brings her dads and extended family to the classroom celebration, where she has more fun than she expected. Her friends and their families accept Stella's family. No one

> says anything about Stella not having a mom at the Mother's Day celebration.
> - Talk to students about how the parts of the story flow from one to the next. Discuss Stella's changes as she goes from being nervous about being the only one without a mother at the party to feeling confident about having two dads and her extended family present for the Mother's Day celebration.
- Invite students to craft or revise their stories so they have a clear beginning, middle, and end.
  - If beginning-middle-end is a tough concept for students, encourage students to tell what happens first, second, next, then, and so on. After students practice writing in the air, encourage them to write on paper after they leave the small-group session.

Power Craft Move:	Structure

Name the craft:	Movement of Time

Why authors do it:	One of a writer's jobs is to keep their story moving along in a way that helps readers understand time is passing.

How to do this:
- Study the way Schiffer uses phrases to help the reader transition through time from scene to scene in the story.
  - On page 13, "The next day . . ."
  - On page 14, "All week . . ."
  - On page 20, "Soon . . ."
  - On page 22, "The big day arrived!"
  - On page 28, "Later that day . . ."
  - Notice that the phrases are set in a different font size, color, and type than the rest of the text.
- Invite students to move readers through time by including short phrases that will help them transition from scene to scene.

Power Craft Move:	Turning Point

Name the craft:	Pivot Point

Why authors do it:	Pivot points are those defining moments when something of great significance happens to the main character and moves the story forward.

How to do this: • Study the turning point in *Stella Brings the Family*.
  • Reread pages 18–23. The turning point takes place when Stella invites Papa, Daddy, and her extended family to the Mother's Day party. She isn't sure if it's the right idea, but she gets to work on the invitations regardless. By page 23, Stella finds the party more wonderful than she even imagined.
  • Invite students to craft or revise the turning point in their stories. Ask students some of the following questions to help them define the turning point.
    • Does the main character undergo any kind of change in order to overcome the story's conflict?
    • Does the main character have a new understanding that changes his or her perspective of everything else that's happened?
    • Does the main character discover a new situation for the first time?

Power Craft Move: Varied Sentence Lengths

Name the craft: Creating Rhythm and Emphasis in Writing

Why authors do it: Varying the lengths of sentences adds life to writing and helps to guide readers.

How to do this: • Study at least two places in *Stella Brings the Family* where Schiffer varies the lengths of sentences. Two possibilities:
  • Reread page 11. The first two sentences are five words long. The third sentence, "Howie had two!," is three words long. Using short sentences may be one way Schiffer encourages readers to stop and think because it's not as commonplace for someone to have two moms. The final sentence on the page contains fourteen words. This long sentence could have been written with more words to make readers feel a sense of urgency as they are rushing through it.
  • Reread pages 29 and 30. The longer sentences on page 29 move readers through the text quickly. But when they turn to page 30, there are only two words on the final page of the book. "Just two" signifies Daddy and Papa, who will be the only guests at the Father's Day party. These final two words, written as a fragment on the final page of text for the book, bring readers to a sudden halt.

- Invite students to vary the sentence lengths in their drafts. Encourage them to craft longer sentences when they want their readers to move along and shorter sentences when they'd like their readers to focus more on the words contained in the short sentences.
  - Tell students that short sentences are powerful because they can provide readers with useful descriptions in quick bursts.

Trouper by Meg Kearney and E. B. Lewis

Publisher's Summary: Trouper ran with a mob of mutts who tipped over trashcans and pawed the cold streets for bones. They howled and cried and wished for a home. Until one day, when the dogs are captured from off the streets and put in cages in a shelter as they wait to be adopted. Trouper watches sadly as, one by one, each of his dog friends are chosen. He's the only one left until finally, one lucky day, just the right boy comes around and finds that this three-legged mutt is the perfect pet for him!

Power Craft Move: Ending

Name the craft: Final Action

Why authors do it: Writers create satisfying endings. One way they do this is by ending with the text and an accompanying illustration that shows a final action.

How to do this:
- Reread pages 28–32.
  - Study the pictures on pages 30–32 with your students. Ask students, "What's going on in these pictures?"
  - Draw attention to the words *play* and *run*. Refer to the running Trouper does with the dogs at the beginning of the story. Ask students how the action of Trouper running with the boy will help readers feel satisfied as they finish the book.
  - Make note of the five footprints in the snow on page 32. Talk about how this detail enhances the feeling readers will have as they experience the final action in the story.
- Invite students to try a final action ending that will leave their readers satisfied as they finish reading.

- Encourage students to look back through their writing in search of actions that matter to the story (just as running with other dogs was important in *Trouper*). Then, they can sketch out possibilities for final action endings in their notebooks.
- Students might create a list of possible actions that will draw their stories to a strong close. From there, students can try crafting endings that illustrate the final action in different ways, sticking with the one that's best.

Power Craft Move:	Lead

Name the craft: Sharing a Secret

Why authors do it: Writers prepare their readers to interact with their texts by crafting strong beginnings. One way they hook their readers is by sharing a secret at the start.

How to do this:
- Reread page 4 of *Trouper*.
- Things you could point out:
  - Kearney takes readers to the past by setting up the "before" time.
  - There is an unexpected action at the end of the sentence. Everything is serene and typical of a dog's life until the final comma. It's as if the narrator, Trouper, is letting the reader in on the secret.
  - Kearney takes readers in a different direction with the story after she writes the final part of the lead.
- Invite students to craft a sharing-a-secret lead.
  - Encourage students to try the same kind of structure Kearney used. Young writers can create a series of four phrases, as Kearney did, and then share a secret with readers in the final part of the sentence.

Power Craft Move:	Punctuation to Create Voice

Name the craft: Dashes

Why authors do it: Writers use dashes to emphasize, interrupt, or change a thought in the middle of a sentence. Dashes can be used to set off part of the text so as to draw attention to it. Sometimes dashes are used to create longer or more dramatic pauses before a page turn.

How to do this:
- Study the following places in the text.
  - Page 19: Hypothesize that the dash was placed there to create a feeling of empathy for Trouper, whose friends are all gone. The illustration and the text work together to evoke emotion. Because of the dash, some readers might linger, wondering how much worse it will get before they turn the page.
  - Page 30: Think aloud about both dashes. They emphasize the phrase "a game called RUN," which appears in the middle of the sentence. The dramatic pause created by the second dash helps to get readers ready for an emotional illustration and description of Trouper's three legs on the final page of the book. There are five footprints, not six, in the snow.
  - Note: There are a few other places dashes are used in the text, but these two spots are similar.
- Invite your students to create dramatic pauses by inserting dashes anywhere they wish to emphasize or draw attention to the text. Writers can employ a dash to create a longer pause anytime they want their readers to linger with a thought or idea.

Power Craft Move: Punctuation to Create Voice

Name the craft: Parentheses

Why authors do it: Sometimes authors add parentheses to clarify something for a reader. Parentheses are also a way of making the writer's voice more conversational.

How to do this:
- Study both places Kearney uses parentheses to share Trouper's thinking in a conversational way. (Parentheses are used only twice in the book, so students shouldn't be inclined to litter their writing with parenthetical references as a result of this lesson.)
  - Reread page 21. The information in the parentheses shows Trouper's internal thinking about places where this kind boy would throw stones. Notice the italicized word, *me,* and talk about the way Trouper and his dog friends have stones

thrown at them on pages 6 and 7. Talk about how the words in the parentheses make you feel empathetic toward Trouper.
- Reread page 24. The parentheses enable Trouper to share information about himself. You might surmise that mentioning that the bowl is black like him makes him feel special. The information in the parentheses reinforces the character's internal thinking, which helps Trouper connect with readers.
- Invite students to insert parentheses sparingly into their writing. Remind them they can include information in parentheses any time they want to get more conversational with their reader—just as Kearney does in *Trouper*.

Power Craft Move:	Punctuation to Create Voice

Name the craft: Semicolon

Why authors do it: Writers separate closely related clauses with semicolons. This adds variety to their writing when they don't want to have several successive choppy sentences that end with periods.

How to do this:
- Study at least two places Kearney uses semicolons to separate closely related ideas in *Trouper*:
  - Reread page 6. Point out all three semicolons. The semicolons highlight the close relationship between the clauses on this page. Kearney might have chosen the semicolon to slow readers down rather than make them stop completely on that page.
  - Reread page 15. The semicolon separates the two main clauses of this sentence. Here the semicolon draws attention to the people staring at the dogs. You might want to talk about the variety of punctuation (semicolon, dash, and commas) if it would be useful to your students. If so, spend time repunctuating this page in advance. Then, talk about how the variety of punctuation marks engages readers.
- Invite students to join related clauses with semicolons anytime they wish to add variety to their writing. Have them scan their drafts for related short sentences that might be joined together with semicolons.

| **Power Craft Move:** | Repetition |

| **Name the craft:** | Repeated Word or Phrase |

Why authors do it: Writers often repeat a word, phrase, or line in order to have a desired effect. Sometimes authors do this several times on a page to create rhythm in the text. Repeating a word also emphasizes something the author would like to have stand out for readers.

How to do this:

- Study places in the text where Kearney repeats the word *before* to create a mood.
  - Reread page 4. Discuss how "before time" makes readers think about the past. The word *before* is repeated four times on this page. Talk to students about how the repetition of the word *before* is powerful, making them think back to the narrator's past life.
  - Reread pages 21 and 23. Have a conversation about what kind of effect Kearney is trying to have on readers by repeating the word *before* many times in the text.
- Invite students to repeat a word or phrase in their writing for emphasis.

| **Power Craft Move:** | Show, Don't Tell |

Name the craft: Draw an Image in the Reader's Mind

Why authors do it: One way writers help readers make a movie in their minds is by using precise language to show their readers what's happening instead of just telling.

How to do this:

- Study at least two places in *Trouper* where Kearney draws an image in the reader's mind to help him or her envision what is happening. Three possibilities:
  - Page 10: The entire page helps readers envision how sad the dogs were when they were locked up at the animal shelter. Instead of Trouper saying, "We didn't like our cages," the author conveys the horrible sounds in the cages. There are four detailed sentences that show, not tell, what it was like to be a locked-up dog.

- Page 23: This is the first time in the text that we learn about Trouper's missing leg. Rather than Kearney telling us he has a missing leg (that E. B. Lewis's pictures show from the beginning of the story), she writes "hairy stump" to show readers that there is something missing. Wonder aloud about the way Trouper leans on people he loves.
- Page 32: Leaving five footprints in the snow requires readers to think about why there aren't six footprints. This page is the only place in the book besides page 23 where we're shown what Trouper looks like through the author's words.
- Invite students to use precise words to show readers what their characters are thinking, feeling, or doing. You might encourage students to elaborate in a way that enhances the deeper meaning of their stories.

Power Craft Move:	Specific Details
Name the craft:	Precise Information
Why authors do it:	Writers know it's important to include precise information about what characters are doing in order to make their writing come alive for their readers.
How to do this:	• Study two places in the text where Kearney includes precise information to help readers envision what is happening in the story.

- Study two places in the text where Kearney includes precise information to help readers envision what is happening in the story.
    - At the end of page 4, "I ran with a mob of mutts." Start by defining *mob* as a loud or disorderly group. Then, have students close their eyes and envision how a mob of mutts would act as opposed to a pack of dogs. Talk about the specific words Kearney chose to help readers envision the way the dogs behave as they travel together.
    - On page 6, Kearney explains the things the mob of mutts did together. She uses specific verbs to show their behavior. Mention some of their actions, like tipping over garbage cans and fighting over pizza scraps. Ask students how these specific details help readers better understand Trouper and the changes he undergoes later in the story.
- Invite students to include precise information about characters in their writing. Encourage students to look for places where they might have summarized and to revise with specific details that will help readers envision what characters are doing.

| **Power Craft Move:** | Structure |

Name the craft: Pacing

Why authors do it: Writers use pacing to control the speed of the text.

How to do this:
- Study places where Kearney varies the pacing of her story.
  - Reread pages 4–6, where Kearney uses specific details, rather than elaborated writing, to share what happened to Trouper before he was caught. Giving readers just enough background information helps them understand that Trouper didn't have an easy or peaceful life in the before time.
  - Show students how pages 10–17 are used to slow down the time Trouper was in the animal shelter. The author uses four page spreads to describe Trouper's tedious life in the shelter before he was chosen.
  - On pages 20 and 21, point out the action, thinking, and dialogue. (Note: This is the only dialogue in the entire book.) Talk about the variety of details on these pages and how Kearney elaborates the scene where the boy selects Trouper to show readers the importance of this moment.
  - Point to the short and medium-length sentences on pages 24, 26, and 28, which move readers through what's happening in Trouper's new home.
  - Pages 30–32 are devoted to running. There are very few words on these pages. This final action happens quickly, but the image of the footprints left behind running through the snow lingers in the reader's mind.
- Invite your students to determine the most important parts of their stories. Embolden them to slow down, as Kearney did, and elaborate for their readers. Encourage them to summarize, with an emphasis on selecting strong words for the parts where they want readers to move faster through their writing.

| **Power Craft Move:** | Turning Point |

Name the craft: Pivot Point

Why authors do it: Pivot points are the defining moments when something happens to the main characters, when they have an epiphany, or when they change in a significant way.

How to do this: • Study the turning point in *Trouper*.

  • Reread pages 19–23. The turning point takes place after all of Trouper's friends leave the animal shelter. The word *until* on page 20 shifts the story in a new direction. The text on page 23 shows that Trouper has found a kid who isn't mean, which changes his perspective on children. Show students how the book's tone shifts when the boy selects Trouper to go home with him.

• Invite students to craft or revise the turning point in their stories. Ask students some of the following questions to help them define it.

  • Does the main character undergo any kind of change in order to overcome the story's conflict?

  • Does the main character have a new understanding that changes his or her perspective?

  • Does the main character make a discovery?

Yard Sale by Eve Bunting and Lauren Castillo

Publisher's Summary: Almost everything Callie's family owns is spread out in their front yard—their furniture, their potted flowers, even Callie's bike. They can't stay in this house, so they're moving to an apartment in the city. The new place is "small but nice," Mom says, and most of their things won't fit, so today they are having a yard sale. But it's kind of hard to watch people buy your stuff, even if you understand why it has to happen. With sensitivity and grace, Eve Bunting and Lauren Castillo portray an event at once familiar and difficult, making clear that a home isn't about what you have, but whom you hold close.

Power Craft Move: Dialogue

Name the craft: Dialogue Advances the Story

Why authors do it: Dialogue is one way writers add details to the plot and expand the relationships between characters while also moving the story forward.

How to do this: • Study two places in *Yard Sale* where Bunting crafts dialogue.

- • Reread pages 16 and 17. There are dialogue tags, as well as sentences that precede and interrupt the dialogue. Including the sentences provides readers with more information while still helping them to understand who is speaking without interrupting the conversation's flow.
- • Reread page 18. Make note of the authentic nature of this conversation between Sara and Callie that sounds like real kids talking. Bunting crafted specific dialogue tags, like *mutters* and *offers,* which make the conversation come alive by helping readers understand how the characters are speaking to one another.
- • Talk with students about the power of dialogue and help them to understand how authors use it to advance their stories.
- • Invite students to add dialogue to places in their stories that will help readers understand what's happening between characters *and* will advance the narrative.
  - • Have students think about real-life conversations. Students can work with partners to write in the air or act out scenes from their stories. Then, ask students to write that dialogue for a given section in a way that will move their stories forward before they head back to their writing spots.

Power Craft Move: Internal Thinking

Name the craft: Creating Characters' Emotional Lives

Why authors do it: Writers use a variety of details to show what's happening to the characters in their story. Internal dialogue is one method that writers use to help readers understand a character's thinking.

How to do this:
- • Study two places in *Yard Sale* where Bunting includes Callie's internal thoughts.
  - • Reread page 6. The final sentence, "But it didn't feel like ours," is Callie's internal thought. Bunting may have included that line to let readers know Callie is feeling uncomfortable about the new home. This internal thought helps a reader gain insight into Callie's feelings, which are different than what she expresses to her parents when she tells them her new bed looks nice.

- Reread page 11. Callie wishes she hadn't put the crayon marks on the bed because it means her family won't get as much money for it. The word *wish* helps the reader understand what Callie is thinking about but not saying.
- Invite students to include internal thinking in their narratives to show what's happening on the inside of their characters.
  - Have students draw their stories across pages or create storyboards. Next, they can add thought bubbles to each part of their stories to show what the characters are thinking and feeling. Have them add the thought bubbles in pencil so they can try out different inner thoughts or reactions for their characters.
  - If students need additional support, pair them with peers and have them role-play by pretending to be their characters. Encourage them to say aloud what their characters might be thinking or feeling. You might need to provide some prompts, such as "I'm really thinking . . . ," "I feel . . . ," or "On the outside I might act like . . . but really I'm thinking. . . ."

Power Craft Move:	Ending

Name the craft: Lesson Learned

Why authors do it: Characters change or grow in stories. One way writers can illustrate their characters' changes is by having them learn a lesson.

How to do this:
- Reread pages 30–32. Study the words and pictures on the page spreads.
  - Point out how Callie has come to terms with the move and the things the family has sold. On page 32, you could highlight the lines "But we will fit in our new place. And we are taking us." This shows Callie's growth as a character and her understanding that it's the people you're with, rather than the things you have, that are most important.
    - Refer back to certain places in the beginning and middle of the story where Callie's feelings about moving are vastly different so students can pinpoint her growth.
- Invite students to show the way in which their characters change by the end of their stories by revealing some of their feelings.

Power Craft Move:	Lead

Name the craft:	Meeting the Characters

Why authors do it: Writers bring readers into the world of the story by introducing the main character immediately.

How to do this:
- Reread pages 4–7 of *Yard Sale*. Some things to point out:
  - *Yard Sale* begins with a feeling of uncertainty for Callie, the main character. We can assume she was told she was moving and she is coming to terms with it in the beginning of the story. She is uncertain whether she's happy about this.
    - It's poignant for Callie to see all her family's possessions spread out on the lawn. We're discovering how she feels about the move in the scene with Callie and her parents when she gets to see the smallness of her new apartment. It doesn't feel right.
  - Readers can also envision the setting by closely examining the illustrations that show a forlorn Callie sitting on the front steps looking at all her family's possessions.
    - Talk about the way this kind of lead made you feel for Callie. The setting is steeped in sadness. Bunting chooses precise words and phrases, including "almost everything" and "all for sale."
- Invite students to bring readers into the world of their stories by introducing the main character (and possibly the secondary characters) from the very first paragraph.
  - Encourage sophisticated writers to think about ways they can infuse the main character's feelings into their writing, which Bunting does through dialogue and internal thinking on page 6.
  - Remind students to include just enough about the characters in the lead of their stories so they draw their readers in without overwhelming them with too many character details.

Power Craft Move:	Punctuation to Create Voice

Name the craft:	Commas

Why authors do it: Writers use commas to help readers figure out which words go together in a sentence. Commas also help readers figure out which parts of a sentence are most important. Writers use commas when they list, add details, and state when or where something happens.

How to do this:
- Study the following examples with students.
  - On page 8, "Today there are a lot of people walking around our front yard, picking up things, asking the price, though Mom and Dad already put prices on them." Start by deconstructing this sentence with students. Commas are used to list (i.e., walking around the yard, picking up things, and asking the price), but they're also used to add more detail. For instance, the sentence would be complete if the word *and* were inserted prior to "asking the price." Suggest Bunting includes "though Mom and Dad already put prices on them" to add more detail to the sentence. Try rewriting the sentence, separating "though Mom and Dad already put prices on them" into its own sentence to show students that it cannot stand on its own. All these ideas are related, which is why Bunting probably opted to construct a long sentence with commas.
  - On page 12, "My best friend, Sara, and her little brother, Petey, come over from their house next door." Including the names of Sara and Petey isn't necessary, but the detail enhances the sentence and gets readers ready for the next few pages. Try rereading the sentence with fewer words, such as "My best friend" *or* "Sara"; "her little brother" *or* "Petey," to help readers understand how more words make this part of the text richer and more detailed.

  - Go to Grammarly's comma-usage page for additional resources on using commas, http://www.grammarly.com/handbook/punctuation/comma/.
- Invite your students to craft longer sentences that are held together with commas in the right places. Encourage them to use commas in lists and whenever they want to elaborate a bit more.

Power Craft Move: Show, Don't Tell

Name the craft: Draw an Image in the Reader's Mind

Why authors do it: One way writers help readers make a movie in their minds is by using precise language to show readers what's happening instead of just telling.

How to do this:
- Study at least two places in *Yard Sale* that show the reader precisely what's occurring. Here are some possibilities:
  - Reread pages 20 and 21. First, study the sentence, "He's pointing at a red geranium in a big blue pot." This description is richer than just "flower pot." The description Bunting uses, brimming with adjectives, helps us picture what the flower pot looks like. Using many adjectives will not necessarily make writing stronger. However, this description helps us understand the conversation that comes on page 21, since it helps us understand how heavy the pot was, which is why the man has to heave it into his truck.
  - Reread page 22. Emphasize the way words like *droopy* and *rubbing* help readers understand how tired Callie's parents are after the yard sale. Instead of saying that the parents are tired, Bunting shows their exhaustion.
  - Reread pages 25 and 26, with a special focus on "A shiver runs through me, from my toes to my head." This sentence is necessary because it shows exactly how uncomfortable the woman's comment made Callie. With this sentence, we get an understanding of how badly Callie feels, which sets us up for the climax of the story. Try restating this sentence in more generic terms so readers can hear why Bunting's version is more powerful.
- Invite students to find places in their writing where they tell the readers what is happening. Encourage them to revise, using precise words to help readers envision what's happening. Remind students to describe how characters' inside stories (their feelings and thoughts) might be different from their outside stories (actions, descriptions, sensory awareness, and conversations).

Step Inside a Small-Group Lesson: Show, Don't Tell with *Yard Sale*

In May 2015, my writing critique group spent an entire session studying the ways Karen Hesse demonstrates the show, don't tell power craft move in *Come On, Rain!* Each of us had spent time studying the text prior to our critique session because we wanted to use Hesse's book as a mentor text for our own writing. This experience reminds me that even adult writers need help emphasizing the show, don't tell concept, so it's no wonder children need multiple exposures to this important craft move to truly understand what it means.

Angie Harrison opened the doors to her third-grade classroom to me while I was writing this book. She was in the midst of transitioning to a writing workshop model during a visit I made in February 2015. Angie had noticed that several of her students were telling, rather than showing, their readers what was happening in their narrative writing. I pulled a small group of students together to help them expand their writing.

Alexandra, Colton, Emma, and Konner came to the carpet with their drafts. Together we studied two places in *Yard Sale* where Eve Bunting shows the reader what is happening. Specifically, we focused on the verbs Bunting chose to use on pages 21 and 22. I decided to make use of Angie's Smart Board. I wrote the sentences on the Smart Board, minus the verbs. Although the students had heard the book read aloud to them before, they didn't know it well enough to remember all the words. To guide them, I asked the students to insert verbs that showed, rather than told, readers what was happening (see Figure 5.3). I encouraged these young writers to select verbs that would help readers envision what the characters were feeling.

Figure 5.3
I wrote down the words students suggested in the blank. Afterward, I showed them the actual word Bunting used in her text.

Next, we discussed the way words like *droopy* and *heaves* help readers envision what is happening in the text. Afterward, I gave the students some sticky notes and invited them to find and mark places in their writing where they told the reader what was happening. They rewrote some of their sentences—showing instead of telling—on the sticky notes so they wouldn't have to recopy their entire text on a new sheet of paper. I reminded them to select precise words to describe how their character was acting, thinking, talking, or feeling.

Emma and Konner were working together on a piece of writing so I invited them up to the whiteboard to try out more descriptive verbs (see Figure 5.4). From there, the two of them went back to their seats and found other places in their text where they needed to show, rather than tell, their readers what was happening to their characters.

Figure 5.4
Emma and Konner use the whiteboard to try their hand at writing descriptive verbs.

Power Craft Move:	Specific Details
Name the craft:	Character Details
Why authors do it:	Writers know it's important to include information about what characters are doing in order to make them seem like real people to their readers.
How to do this:	• Study the characters at three points in *Yard Sale*.

     • On page 15, reread the first paragraph, making note of the second sentence. While Callie tells us she's really angry, we get to see how she handles her rage when she runs over to the man and grabs one of the bike's wheels. Bunting uses action, description, and dialogue to convey Callie's discontent. Help students understand that these strings of details make readers empathize with the main character.

- On page 16, readers learn more about Dad. Reread the text and talk with students about the way the details work together to help us understand Dad's character. We learn he's comforting to his daughter with the gentle way he handles the dispute she's having with the man about the bike. We learn he's also sad but is trying not to show it in front of his daughter.
- On page 18, we discover little details about the way Sara smells (like Fruit Loops) and how she puts Petey's pacifier back into his mouth as soon as it falls out. We also hear Sara offer to ask her parents if Callie could stay with them. These details work together to create the picture of a little girl.

- Invite students to include pertinent character details in their writing by thinking about aspects of their main and secondary characters. Encourage students to look for places where they can embed details about their characters that will help readers get to know the kind of people they are.

Power Craft Move:	Structure
Name the craft:	Movement of Time
Why authors do it:	One of a writer's jobs is to keep the story moving along in a way that helps readers understand time is passing. Writers craft sentences that move their readers from scene to scene in their writing.
How to do this:	• Study the following places in *Yard Sale* so you can talk with students about the way we move through time in the story.

- Study the following places in *Yard Sale* so you can talk with students about the way we move through time in the story.
  - Reread page 12 and study the illustration on page 13. Notice the following things aloud:
    - It's early in the day because Sara and Petey are both wearing pajamas.
    - Sara remarks about the number of people who turned out at the yard sale.
    - The balloons are flying high on the mailbox.
    - There are many items available for sale.
  - Reread the text on page 22 and study the illustration on page 23. Suggest the following:

- • Sara and Petey are heading toward their house.
- • There are fewer people at the sale.
- • The balloons are sagging.
- • Callie tells us nearly everything has been sold and what's left is being sold for less money.
- • Reread the text on page 28 and study the illustration on pages 28 and 29. Point out:
  - • There are few people left at the yard sale.
  - • The balloons are lying on the ground.
  - • Dad has declared everything that's left is free.
- • Ask students to think about the ways the author and illustrator moved readers through time with small details. Then debrief and share.
- • Invite students to move readers through time by including small yet relevant details that will move readers from scene to scene in their writing.

Power Craft Move:	Turning Point

Name the craft: Pivot Point

Why authors do it: Pivot points are those defining moments when something of great significance happens to the main character. A turning point moves the story forward when the main character changes in a significant way.

How to do this:
- • Study the turning point in *The Yard Sale*.
  - • Reread pages 25 and 26. The turning point takes place when the older woman at the yard sale asks Callie if she's for sale. Suggest Bunting chose an emotional moment to send Callie into tears, driving home the big message of the story for readers. Talk about the importance of this scene and how Callie comes to realize how important she is to her parents as they comfort her. Bunting shows Callie touching at least one of her parents from this point in the story onward, instead of the way she is often pictured by herself prior to the turning point. Talk about the way Castillo's illustrations enhance the story's bigger message about family relationships being more important than material items.

- Tip: You might think aloud about ways Bunting could have communicated this closeness to readers if her text didn't have an illustrator.
- Invite students to create a story mountain to help them find the turning point of their narrative. Creating a story mountain will help students build tension for their characters as they meet and overcome difficulty.
  - If students have not created a story mountain in the past, show them a prepared story mountain for *Yard Sale* that illustrates the rising slope. Make note of where the story starts and how it begins not too far away from the "top" of the mountain.

Power Craft Move:	Varied Sentence Lengths

Name the craft: Creating Rhythm and Emphasis in Writing

Why authors do it: Writers vary the length of their sentences in order to communicate meaning and tone to their readers and because it can make writing more interesting to read.

How to do this:
- Study two places in *Yard Sale* where Bunting varies the lengths of sentences.
  - On page 11, there's a combination of dialogue, simple sentences, and longer sentences. Attend to the punctuation while rereading the sentences so students can pay attention to the way punctuation acts like stage directions (Feigelson 2008) telling your voice what to do as a reader. Explain what you're noticing about the places where sentences are shorter and where they're longer. Help students understand how sentence length contributes to the mood of this page.
  - On page 28, there are a variety of sentence lengths. Draw students' attention to the sentence Dad says aloud, which has a longer sentence, a fragment, and then a short sentence. The use of the fragment and the shorter sentence command readers to stop and think about the message Dad was trying to send to the people milling about. It reads as if it's his stream of consciousness, with a little more information coming out with every sentence.

- Invite students to vary the sentence lengths in their drafts. Encourage them to craft longer sentences when they want their readers to move right along and shorter sentences when they'd like their readers to focus more on the words contained in the short sentences.

6 Nonfiction Lesson Sets: Moving from Narrative to Informational Writing

Although they're only six and seven years old, first graders know about lots of things! They can bring their life experiences to an "all-about" book unit of study and share their knowledge with readers. However, I noticed that some of the first graders I worked with while writing this book had a tough time switching gears from their storytelling voices to the more authoritative voice that informational writing requires.

I read *The Slug* aloud to Kelly Sherbo's first-grade students during one of my classroom visits in winter 2015. Later, I used it as a mentor text when I worked with small groups of her students. Kelly's first graders were engaged in the Nonfiction Chapter Books unit of study, which was the second unit of the school year. (They had previously written small-moment stories.) Alex, Ashleigh, Evan, and Jordana arrived for the strategy lesson with their second stapled book of the unit in hand. Each of their books read more like a narrative than an informational piece.

I used *The Slug* to teach them how nonfiction craft writing teaches readers about a big topic. We first studied pages 10–13, which focus on the slug's tentacles, and then we studied pages 18–25, which explain mucus. Afterward, I debriefed, asking the students if they had noticed how Gravel groups all the information on the pages around a given topic. Next, I asked them to brainstorm a list of things they could teach someone, such as the categories they had chosen for their books. Each student created a short list and then returned to his or her seat to write about those aspects of the topic. For instance, Jordana's list included training horses, where horses live, what horses eat, and how to care for horses.

The next time I visited Kelly's classroom, I met with Jordana again. She showed me her completed book about horses, which reflected the categorizing work we had done during my previous visit (see a page from her book in Figure 6.1). I noticed that on each page she had included a page header that corresponded to the true table of contents she eventually put together for her book. When we conferred, Jordana said she was proud of herself for staying focused on one topic on each page. I was impressed, too!

Figure 6.1
Jordana's book about horses shows her ability to organize information gathered for nonfiction writing.

	Back Matter	Content-Specific Vocabulary	Lead/Ending	Precise Words	Punctuation to Create Voice	Quotes and Sources	Repetition	Teaching Tone	Text Features	Topics and Sub-topics
A Rock Is Lively		x	x	x	x				x	x
A Splash of Red	x		x	x	x	x	x			
Big Red Kangaroo	x	x	x	x	x			x		
Coral Reefs		x	x	x	x				x	x
Elizabeth, Queen of the Seas	x		x	x	x		x		x	
Founding Mothers		x	x	x	x	x		x	x	x
I See a Pattern Here	x	x	x					x	x	x
No Monkeys, No Chocolate	x	x	x	x				x	x	x
See What a Seal Can Do	x	x	x			x		x	x	
The Slug		x	x	x				x	x	x

Figure 6.2

Ten nonfiction mentor texts and their power craft moves

About the Lesson Sets

Figure 6.2 shows the power craft moves supported by the ten mentor texts for nonfiction writing. I have included at least six power craft lessons for each of the featured books. As mentioned in Chapter 5, you will notice that some power craft moves are featured in multiple texts. I did this because your grade-level or content-area curriculum might dictate which nonfiction books you purchase. In addition, you might need to teach a series of strategy lessons to groups of young writers so they can master the craft. Although you may use different books, the similar format of the lessons will help your students become familiar with the process.

Diversity in Nonfiction

The We Need Diverse Books organization comprises children's literature enthusiasts who advocate for "essential changes in the publishing industry to produce and promote literature that reflects and honors the lives of all young people" (2015). As one of the many children's book lovers who support the We Need Diverse Books mission, I believe it's equally important to have diversity in nonfiction texts. The selections in this chapter include *A Splash of Red*, the biography of an African American artist and World War I veteran; *Big Red Kangaroo*, a journey to the wilds of Australia; and *Founding Mothers,* which celebrates the women who played an influential role in establishing the United States. I hope some of these nonfiction books will provide your students with opportunities to look at the world in different ways.

A Rock Is Lively by Dianna Hutts Aston and Sylvia Long

Publisher's Summary: From the award-winning creators of *An Egg Is Quiet, A Seed Is Sleepy, A Butterfly Is Patient,* and *A Nest Is Noisy* comes a gorgeous and informative introduction to the fascinating world of rocks. From dazzling blue lapis lazuli to volcanic snowflake obsidian, an incredible variety of rocks are showcased in all their splendor. Poetic in voice and elegant in design, this book introduces an array of facts, making it equally perfect for classroom sharing and family reading.

Power Craft Move: Content-Specific Vocabulary

Name the craft: Technical Language Teaches Readers About Topics

Why authors do it: Nonfiction writers infuse their writing with technical language to teach their readers more about a topic. The technical language a writer chooses must be defined for a reader. Writers often use commas to offset the definitions of words they define in context.

How to do this:
- Study at least two places in *A Rock Is Lively* where Aston uses commas to offset the definitions of words. Two possibilities:
  - Reread page 20. In order to explain the height of Mount Augustus, Aston uses the word *elevation.* Hypothesize that Aston probably knows some of her readers won't recognize the word, so she writes, "an *elevation,* or height, of 3,628 feet." Teach your students that they may use the word repeatedly once they define it, without defining it again.
  - Reread the sentence containing "erosion" on page 33. Aston shows the process of erosion. This helps readers understand how it happens over time.
- Point out how Aston italicizes words she defines and offsets them with commas.

- Invite students to use technical language to teach their readers about a topic. Encourage students to define a technical term in context, using commas to offset the definition.

Power Craft Move:	Ending

Name the craft:	Circular Ending

Why authors do it:	A circular ending brings the writing back to where it began.

How to do this:
- Reread pages 10–13, which assert that rocks are lively. Next, jump forward to pages 32–35, where readers learn how a rock is recycled. Pages 32–33 summarize the process of erosion, but the circular ending (pages 33–34) reinforces the lively nature of rocks.
- Invite students to craft a circular ending. Encourage them to review the beginning of their writing and ask, "Can I end my writing by coming full circle as Aston did?"

Power Craft Move:	Lead

Name the craft:	Simile

Why authors do it:	Writers may begin with a rich description that compares two unlike things.

How to do this:
- Study pages 10–13 with students.
  - Aston employs a simile, comparing a rock to a pot of soup that is deep below the surface of the earth. He uses words such as *liquid* and *boiling* to make the image more lifelike.
- Invite students to craft a simile lead of their own. They might start by brainstorming a word bank of things they could compare to their subjects. Remind them to use rich description to make their simile believable to readers.

Power Craft Move:	Precise Words

Name the craft:	Vivid Verbs

Why authors do it:	Selecting the right words is just as important when you're writing nonfiction as it is when you're writing fictional narratives. Verbs are perhaps the most important part of a sentence because they show what is happening.

How to do this: • Study two places in the text where the author uses vivid verbs. Here are two possibilities:
- On page 19, reread the sentence and explain what *ingests* means. Hypothesize about why Aston chose the word (e.g., *ingests* helps readers create a picture in their minds).
- On page 32, reread the sentence where "erupts" appears and define it. Explain how the word *erupts* is stronger than writing "breaks through." Discuss how you can envision the word *erupts* in your mind.
- Invite students to edit their writing. Encourage them to use verbs that will help their writing come to life.
  - Remind students to stretch themselves by using bigger words they know, rather than consulting a thesaurus. Have them read their new sentences aloud to make sure their new verbs accurately reflect the context.

Power Craft Move: Punctuation to Create Voice

Name the craft: Inside Dashes

Why authors do it: When nonfiction writers craft texts, they tuck in important information to teach their readers as much possible about a topic. Aston provides extra information inside dashes. Dashes are used like commas in this book.

How to do this: • Study two places in *A Rock Is Lively* where Aston used dashes.
- On page 17, Aston teaches about comets. Read the sentence twice to students and note how Aston includes some additional information about an informal term for comets. Hypothesize how Aston must have thought this was something else she could teach readers about comets.
- On page 25, Aston used dashes to interrupt her writing about geodes. Read the sentence twice with students and note how Aston includes more information to help readers get a better picture in their minds about geodes. Talk about how the extra information contained inside the dashes helps readers understand what the geode looks like and where it is found.
- Invite students to examine one of their paragraphs that could benefit from using dashes to include a deeper explanation for readers. Encourage students to revise a paragraph using dashes, as Aston does. If they have additional information, encourage them to craft a new sentence using dashes to section off the new details.

Power Craft Move:	Text Features

Name the craft: Headings

Why authors do it: Nonfiction writers use headings to introduce categories to readers. By naming a category with a heading, writers tell readers what the words and drawings on the page will mostly be about. The heading is like the main idea and everything that follows is supporting information.

How to do this:
- Examine two page spreads in the text with headings:
  - On pages 24 and 25, the heading is "A rock is surprising." Think aloud about what you'd expect to learn on these two pages. Reread the text and examine the illustrations to determine if you learn something surprising about rocks on these pages. Make note of how illustrations and writing work together to teach us about the main idea in the heading.
  - On pages 28 and 29, the heading is "A rock is creative." This time invite students to state what they'd expect to learn from these pages. Reread the pages and ask students to turn and talk about how the words and illustrations work together to support the idea that "a rock is creative."
- Some students may benefit from explicitly learning that headings are like the main idea. You can tell them that headings give readers clues about what they're going to learn.
- Invite students to write the headings for each category of their informational books. Like Aston, they could craft headings that are sentences. (For instance, students can use their topic and repeat it over and over again, page after page. Then, the end of the sentence will change based on the information in each category.) Encourage students to try writing a few headings while they're working with you. Have students share what they come up with before sending them back to their independent writing spots.

Power Craft Move:	Text Features

Name the craft: Print Layout

Why authors do it: When writing an informational book, it's important to think about how to present information to readers. One thing writers and illustrators think about is the way they will present information on each page.

How to do this: • Examine some page spreads from *A Rock Is Lively* that contain an unusual print layout. Here are some places to examine with students:

- On pages 10 and 11, point out how the author uses just four words, which are also the title of the book, followed by ellipsis points. Discuss the illustrations contained in the spread.
- On pages 12 and 13, notice three more dots, or ellipsis points, that finish the thought from the previous page: " . . . bubbling like a pot of soup deep beneath the earth's crust . . . liquid . . . molten . . . boiling." Ask students to hypothesize about why the author separates the full sentence on two separate page spreads. Talk about the purposeful ways the writer and illustrator want readers to consider the writing and illustrations being presented.
- On pages 20 and 21, the heading spans both pages. Point out that the illustration of the Mount Augustus, often known as the world's largest rock, spans the top of the page spread. There are many tiny rocks, shown underneath a magnifying glass, on the bottom of the recto page. Perhaps the heading was placed over two pages to make readers look in different spots for it, just as one has to look in different places on the page for the illustrations to which the heading refers. Talk about how the opposite placement may reflect the opposites (huge and tiny) in the text of this page spread.

• Invite students to decide how to structure the pages in their informational books. Encourage them to lay out most of the pages in their informational books in the same way. However, they may choose to present a few pages in a unique way so it will support the writing.

- Encourage students to pick a page that could benefit from a unique layout, like the ones you studied in *A Rock Is Lively*.
- Remind them that the layout must function as a teaching tool for readers, not just look funky.

Power Craft Move: Topics and Subtopics

Name the craft: Creating Categories

Why authors do it: One way many authors break up their topics is by thinking of subtopics or categories for their writing.

How to do this:
- Study at least two places in the text where Aston created categories. Here are two possibilities:
  - Pages 16 and 17 start with the heading "A rock is galactic." Point out that all the information on these pages is about rocks found in outer space.
    - Meteoroids, comets, and asteroids are interesting and might have had a page of their own. Posit that Aston groups them because they fall into the same category: rocks that can be found only in outer space.
  - Pages 32 and 33 begin with the heading "A rock is recycled." Show students that all the information on these pages is about rocks that began in different forms and changed over time.
    - Note that Aston discusses three specific types of rocks: sedimentary, metamorphic, and igneous rocks. All these rocks change, which could be why she classifies them under the category "recycled."
  - Some students may note that each page spread contains information categorized around one subtopic (i.e., each page spread provides related information that helps readers learn more about the big topic).
- Invite students to divide their information into different categories so they can teach readers about the big topic.
  - Encourage them to think about all the different aspects of their topics.
    - Provide time for students to jot down several categories before they return to their seats to look through their note cards and sort them into categories.
    - Some students may not have enough notes about a category. Encourage them to do more research, freewrite in their writer's notebook about that category, or delete a category.

Power Craft Move: Topics and Subtopics

Name the craft: Grouping Related Information and Illustrations

Why authors do it: Nonfiction writers teach readers about a big topic. In *A Rock Is Lively*, Aston had to create categories to teach readers all about rocks. Writers create categories by grouping related information and illustrations when they're writing an informational book.

How to do this:

- Study at least two places in *A Rock Is Lively* where Aston groups related information and illustrations. Here are two places to examine with students:
  - On pages 18 and 19, the heading says, "A rock is old," which gets you ready to read all about old rocks. Talk about the text and illustrations that support the idea that "a rock is old." Surmise that age or old rocks is one of Aston's categories.
  - On pages 22 and 23, the heading says, "A rock is helpful." Note that as a reader, you may expect to learn about how rocks can help us do things. Go around the page and talk about how rocks help animals do things. For example, birds swallow stones to *help* them digest food. Note that all the writing and illustrations support the big idea.
- Invite students to narrow the information they've collected. Have them divide their knowledge into different categories and then group related information and drawings as they're writing.

A Splash of Red: The Life and Art of Horace Pippin by Jen Bryant and Melissa Sweet

Publisher's Summary: As a child in the late 1800s, Horace Pippin loved to draw: *He loved the feel of the charcoal as it slid across the floor. He loved looking at something in the room and making it come alive again in front of him.* He drew pictures for his sisters, his classmates, his co-workers. Even during World War I, Horace filled his notebooks with drawings from the trenches . . . until he was shot. Upon his return home, Horace couldn't lift his right arm, and couldn't make any art. Slowly, with lots of practice, he regained use of his arm, until once again, he was able to paint—and paint, and paint! Soon, people—including the famous painter N. C. Wyeth—started noticing Horace's art, and before long, his paintings were displayed in galleries and museums across the country.

Power Craft Move: Back Matter

Name the craft: Historical Note

Why authors do it: Biographers craft stories about people. They make decisions about the kind of information they'll include to ensure that the biography will be interesting to readers. Sometimes they have to determine which details are important enough for the main text and which are better suited as back matter. Historical notes give readers additional information, or the backstory, on a person's life at the conclusion of a biography.

How to do this:
- Reread the historical note on page 35. Invite students to reflect on the kinds of additional information they learn about Horace from the historical note.
  - Some things to point out while you're reading the historical note:
    - Horace won a Purple Heart in World War I.
    - *The End of the War: Starting Home,* the painting that took him three years to complete, was physical and psychological therapy for him.
    - Horace created about 140 works of art.
    - Museums around the country display his artwork.
  - The historical note was another way for Bryant to include interesting information, or the backstory, about Horace into this book. Because everything can't fit into the picture book about Horace, she saved some important facts for the historical note.
  - Help your students figure out what is important for the main body of work and what should be left for a historical note.
- Invite students to sort through their note cards to determine what they want to tell in the main biography and which facts might not fit with the story. Students can create two piles: *fits with the story I'm telling* and *fits in the historical note.* From there, students can write about some of the facts to include in the historical note that will follow the main text.

Power Craft Move: Ending

Name the craft: The Way We Are Known

Why authors do it: Writers often end their writing by focusing on the major accomplishments, qualities, or attributes of the person, object, or animal featured in their writing.

How to do this:
- Reread pages 32 and 33 with your students. The book comes to an end right after we learn that Horace became a famous artist.

The book doesn't end with a lot of fanfare, but rather on an ordinary night when Horace is painting inside his house. Bryant allows us to witness Horace working diligently despite his fame, suggesting that he was still devoted to his art.

- Point out that Horace was known for his art. We see him engaged in his passion on the final page of the book.
- Tip: Remind readers that writing endings is hard. They might need to write several endings to get one that's just right.

- Invite your small group to think about the most important thing about the subjects of their writing. Ask them, "What are they known for?" Then, encourage them to do some jotting in their writer's notebooks to try to write an ending that will help readers remember the essence of their subjects. Students can use the jottings to create the final paragraph of their writing, which will help readers to remember what is most important about their subjects.

Power Craft Move:	Lead

Name the craft: Developing Setting: Creating a Sense of Era

Why authors do it: Writers craft leads that tell more than where the writing takes place. Some writers develop a sense of era by helping readers understand when their narrative takes place. Writers can create a sense of era by using dates and describing events happening at that time.

How to do this:
- Study the text and illustration on page 5 with your students. Point out the following:
  - The date or Horace's birth coincided with President George Washington's birthday, which was considered a day of remembrance after the death of President Washington. There's a sketch of George Washington with the words "Happy birthday George" atop the page.
    - Americans celebrate Presidents Day, which was established in 1885 to recognize the February 22 birthday of President Washington (http://www.history.com/topics/holidays/presidents-day).
  - Readers can interpret the illustration of the small house as a way of understanding that Horace was born at home rather than in a hospital, which would be more in keeping with the late 1800s.

- Ask students: How do the text and illustrations help you picture when and where *A Splash of Red* takes place?
- Invite students to develop a sense of place and era for their readers.
  - Tip: Less experienced writers might want to use the text on page 5 of *A Splash of Red* as a template of sorts to help do more than state the *where* and the *when* in their introductory paragraph.

Step Inside a Small-Group Lesson: Writing Leads with *A Splash of Red*

Many young writers struggle with how to lead off their writing so as to engage their readers. Often you'll see the same kind of lead in students' writing that their teacher uses in the mini-lesson. Although it may be nice to have students personalize the lead, this doesn't encourage variety (when you read the papers) or ownership. What does? Mining mentor texts for strong leads!

In November 2014, I spent time in Meg Rusanowsky's third-grade classroom. Her students were writing short biographies about each other. (Note: Meg's school didn't use writing workshop so it wasn't a biography unit of study per se.) Meg provided students with strategies for interviewing and notetaking. I saw the tracks of her teaching when I met with a small group of students who had categorized their information. However, all the students' drafts seemed to start the same way: a regurgitation of facts about their subject's birth and childhood.

Studying the craft moves authors make is similar to the way we learn how to do something new. For instance, when I wanted to learn how to cut an avocado, I learned by watching someone on a cooking show. I learned about halving the avocado, using a sharp knife to remove the pit, scoring the flesh without piercing the avocado's skin, and scooping it out of the skin. If I were leading a mini-lesson about this process, I might show a short YouTube clip of someone slicing an avocado.

To show Meg's students how to write engaging leads for their biographies, I taught a strategy lesson using *A Splash of Red* by Jen Bryant and Melissa Sweet. We looked closely at the way Jen Bryant began the story of Horace Pippin's life. We reread the first two pages of the book where Bryant begins the story:

On February 22, 1888, the town of West Chester, Pennsylvania, celebrated a holiday. That day, in the same town, Daniel and Christine Pippin celebrated the birth of their son, Horace.

Next, I unpacked these two sentences, noticing these attributes:

- The first sentence includes the date and place of birth.
- The first sentence also mentions a holiday.
- The second sentence has a short phrase followed by a comma, and references the town.
- The second sentence names the parents and tells who was born.
- There is a comma before Horace's name.

I told the young writers that instead of just rattling off facts, they could study Bryant's lead and leads from other biographies. One of the kids dropped her pencil, despondent. "It wasn't a holiday the day my person was born."

Aha, a wonderful teachable moment! We discussed the importance of asking a question such as, "What did this author do to craft this lead that I can do with my own lead?" rather than just recopying the words an author wrote. In the end, Meg's students decided to emulate Bryant's style by crafting new leads with a similar structure. Figure 6.3 shows one student's original lead paragraph and Figure 6.4 shows the revision, which mirrors the mentor text.

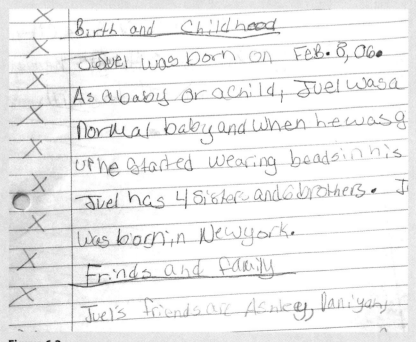

Figure 6.3
This is one student's original lead for a biography.

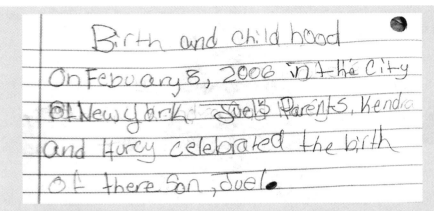

Birth and child hood
On February 8, 2006 in the City
of New York Juel's Parents, Kendra
and Hurcy celebrated the birth
of there Son, Juel.

Figure 6.4
Using *A Splash of Red* as a mentor text, the student revised her original lead, shown in Figure 6.3, to a narrative style.

As students revised their leads, I reminded them that as they worked on their drafts, they could continue to examine texts like *A Splash of Red* and pay attention to the way authors present information to make their writing interesting for others to read.

After teaching this small-group lesson, I realized I could do more with the lead from *A Splash of Red*. Instead of only using it as a template, I could use it as an example of how some authors develop a sense of place and era when sharing their research.

Power Craft Move:	Precise Words
Name the craft:	Vivid Verbs
Why authors do it:	Vivid verbs show readers precisely what is happening in a piece of writing.
How to do this:	• Study at least two of the following places in the text.

- • On page 7, "He sorted laundry with his sisters." The word *sorted* helps readers to picture Horace separating the clean clothes into neatly folded piles.
- • On page 16, "He wrapped his hands around a rifle." The word *wrapped* helps readers to envision Horace's large hands around the barrel of a gun.
- • On page 24, "Using his good arm to move the hurt one, he scorched lines into the wood." The word *scorched* helps readers to see how he moved his arm to burn pictures into the wood.

- Talk about how these vivid words are more powerful than more vague words.
- Invite students to find places in their writing in need of stronger verbs. Encourage them to look for spots where they want to strengthen the picture readers will make in their minds.

Power Craft Move: Punctuation to Create Voice

Name the craft: Colon, Then Commas in a List

Why authors do it: Writers can use colons to introduce lists after they have written a complete sentence. Introduce a list with a colon *only if* the words that precede it can stand alone.

How to do this:
- Study at least one place in *A Splash of Red* where Bryant uses a colon and then commas in a list.
  - On page 13, reread the part that begins with "For several years." Reread the first line, "For several years, Horace's big hands were *always* busy," to reinforce that the section can stand as its own sentence. Bryant uses a colon to alert readers to the list of related things (that Horace did with his hands) that follows.
  - On page 21, reread the entire page. All the text that precedes the colon is a complete sentence. Like the other example, Bryant alerts readers that a list of related things is coming by using a colon to help readers understand all the things Horace wanted to draw.
- Invite students to find a list in their writing they can revise, using Bryant's text as a mentor. If students don't have a list, encourage them to look back through their note cards to find information they could use in this same manner.

Power Craft Move: Punctuation to Create Voice

Name the craft: Ellipses Points

Why authors do it: Many authors use ellipses when they want a character's voice to trail off or when they want to show what a character is thinking. There are additional ways to use ellipses. For example, in *A Splash of Red*, Bryant uses ellipses to close some sentences.

How to do this:
- Study both places in the text where the author uses ellipses in this way:
  - Reread the second paragraph on page 9. Surmise that Bryant wants to lead readers into the next sentence slowly. Or maybe she wants readers to pause because she is trying to be humorous. Ask students what would happen if they were caught doodling during a spelling test.
  - Reread the text on the bottom of page 18. Talk about Horace's injury being tragic. Wonder aloud that Bryant may have used the ellipsis to make readers stop and think about what would happen the next time someone asked Horace to make a picture for them. With his arm injured, would he still be able to create art?
  - Spend a moment recapping the similarities and differences in the two examples of ellipses.
- Invite students to examine their writing to find one or two places they'd like readers to linger a bit before showing them what is going to happen next. Encourage them to use ellipses to help readers stop and think before leading them to the next sentence.

Power Craft Move: Quotes and Sources

Name the craft: Citations

Why authors do it: Responsible writers always cite passages, quotes, or sources referenced in their work. They do this to properly document material that isn't their own and to help their readers know from where material originally came.

How to do this:
- Study the way Bryant attributes the quotes she uses from Horace Pippin throughout *A Splash of Red*. Here are two examples:
  - Read aloud the first quote on page 36, which includes the name of the book in italics, followed by the page numbers. Explain to students that including this information can help a reader go to the source.
  - Read aloud the fifth quote on page 36. Ask students to examine the citation that follows the quote and name the source, *Horace Pippin: A Negro Painter in America*. Note that Bryant lists the page number along with other important publication information. It is worth reiterating that this will help

someone read more about the context of Pippin's original quote.

- Talk with the group about *why* Bryant may have included these quotation sources in her book. Do they think she was trying to help readers extend their investigation, or was she trying to teach young writers the importance of noting where they find information?

- Invite your students to look back through their note cards and make sure they've written the title and author of each source they've used as a reference and have written down the page number of any quotation they copied from a book. If not, they should locate the sources now. Remind students that if they properly cite information as they collect it, they will have an easier time compiling the source list for the biography they're crafting.

Power Craft Move:	Repetition
Name the craft:	Power of Three
Why authors do it:	Sometimes writers use the repetition of a word, phrase, or action three times to draw attention to something in the text. Many people believe that three repetitions of something in writing make the writing funnier, more memorable, or more satisfying to the reader.
How to do this:	• Study two places in the text where Bryant uses the power of three.

- Study two places in the text where Bryant uses the power of three.
  - Reread the bottom of page 20 where Bryant explains some of the odd jobs Horace took when he came home from the war with an arm injury. We learned he organized a Boy Scout troop, umpired baseball games, and took kids fishing. There's a difference between these jobs (mind based) and how they differ from what Horace used to do (with his hands).
  - Reread page 33, which is the final page of the book. Discuss why you think Bryant chose to use the power of three to close the story. If students need help, suggest how it creates a vivid picture of him in the reader's mind. Some students might notice that the three strong images enable them to envision what Horace looked like as he approached a canvas. Perhaps it was to help readers understand the struggle he continued to face as he persevered to create art. All interpretations should be welcomed.

- Invite students to find at least one place in their writing where they'd like to call their reader's attention to something by using the power of three.

Power Craft Move:	Repetition
Name the craft:	Refrain
Why authors do it:	Writers highlight lines throughout their texts to showcase a particularly strong idea. Repeating a line at several points during a piece of writing is called a refrain and can help readers come away with the big idea or message.
How to do this:	• Jen Bryant uses a refrain that varies slightly throughout the text. It's a variation of "Make a picture for us, Horace!" on pages 9, 12, 14, 16, 18, and 24. I'd suggest rereading this line with students to show them how it evolves throughout the book. For example, it disappears between pages 18 and 24 (until Horace finds a way to create art again).

- Invite students to reread their drafts.
  - They might find a line that could be repeated a few times across their text. If so, they should add it throughout their piece, as Bryant did, to strengthen their writing.
  - If they don't find a line they can repeat throughout their writing, invite them to craft one. Encourage students to write a short sentence, as Bryant did, to emphasize a big idea they want their readers to understand by repeating throughout the text.

Big Red Kangaroo by Claire Saxby and Graham Byrne

Publisher's Summary: In the center of Australia, the sun is setting over the baked earth, and Red Kangaroo stirs from his rest. It's breakfast time, and Red must lead his mob of kangaroos off to find grasses for grazing. But Red is also on the watch for young male kangaroos who are ready to challenge him and try to take his place as leader. Striking illustrations set the mood for a compelling, fact-filled story of red kangaroos in the wilds of Australia.

Power Craft Move:	Back Matter

Name the craft:	Information Page

Why authors do it:	Some authors write narrative nonfiction, which are stories about animals or real-life events. Sometimes the stories follow the exact sequence of events and sometimes they're embellished. Writers often include an informational page at the end of their text to share additional facts about the subjects.

How to do this:

- Reread page 23. Use your fingers to retell the new information you learned about red kangaroos. Some examples:
    - Kangaroos are marsupials.
    - Red Kangaroos are the largest macropods.
    - Red Kangaroos reside in areas where food and water are scarce.
- Hypothesize about why some of this general information about red kangaroos is included in the back matter rather than embedded in the main text. Help students figure out what may be important for the main body of work versus what is included on the informational page.
- Invite students to review their note cards to determine which information is most important to include in the body of their writing and which information could merely be noted at the end. Students can create two piles: *fits with the majority of the writing I'm doing* and *works better as back matter*. From there, students can write up some of the facts about their subject matter for inclusion on a separate general information page that will reside behind the main text they're composing.

Power Craft Move:	Content-Specific Vocabulary

Name the craft:	Content-Specific Words

Why authors do it:	Writers find and use the right words that help their readers understand the topic. Often, content-specific words are defined in context, in a sidebar, or in a book's glossary.

How to do this:

- Study at least two of the following places in *Big Red Kangaroo* where Saxby embeds content-specific language:

- Reread the second paragraph on page 2 and all of page 3, which explains the word *mobs.* Show readers that the definition of a mob can be found in the first sentence of page 3 (i.e., "Red kangaroos live in families called mobs."). Show readers how the information on pages 2 and 3 helps them to understand who else lives in a red kangaroo's mob (i.e., at least one other female and several joeys).
- Reread page 15 through the lens of figuring out the meaning of the word *predators,* which is used but not defined. Based on the information about goannas and dingoes, ask students, "Do you understand what the word *predators* means on this page?" If it's unclear, you might rewrite the first sentence of page 15 together to include a comma followed by the words *an animal that lives by eating other animals.* (If you rewrite this sentence, remind students of the importance of including the definition for readers within the text.)
- Reread the regular and italicized text on page 17 focusing on the word *challenge.* Readers can understand that *challenge* means to confront physically by reading the sentences around it and looking at the illustrations. Talk about the specificity of the word *challenge* and how it is used in other forms, such as *challenger,* on page 17 and beyond.
- Reread the italicized text on page 19 focusing on the word *dominance.* (If necessary, refer to page 3, where the word *dominant* is initially used to refer to the dominant male of a mob.) Help readers understand that dominance is the fight for influence or control of the mob. You can help readers understand the significance of this word by examining the rest of the text on the page and by using the illustrations to help.
- Invite students to use content-specific words to help readers understand the subject matter. Remind students that it is helpful to readers when the definitions can be found in the text. (For instance, it's easier to understand the meaning of *mobs* than *dominance* since *mobs* is defined on the page.) Encourage students to create drawings to enhance the meaning of content-specific words as Byrne does on pages 16 and 18.

Power Craft Move:	Ending

Name the craft:	Wondering Ending

Why authors do it: Writers wrap up their stories in a way that leaves room for readers to ponder what will happen in the future.

How to do this:

- Reread pages 20 and 21 to your students. Show them how the regular and italicized text complement each other. That is, the text on page 20 ends with the words "For now," which make one wonder what will happen next. The italicized text on page 21 confirms that the mob will follow a new leader if the male loses the next challenge. Even though Saxby wraps up Red and his mob's day on page 20, she leaves readers with the notion that it's uncertain whether Red will remain in control of his mob with the words "For now" and with the information presented on page 21.
  - There are lingering thoughts and unanswered questions in this ending. For now, readers can imagine the possibilities: what might happen next and what might remain the same. Readers have to conclude that things in nature are always changing; they have to wonder how long Red and his mob will stay safe.
- Invite students to draft a wondering ending where they wrap up most of their story but leave something uncertain for their readers. Encourage them to leave something unresolved or fore-boding, as Saxby does on page 20 of *Big Red Kangaroo*.

Power Craft Move:	Lead

Name the craft:	Meeting the Characters

Why authors do it: Even in nonfiction writing, authors bring readers into the world of the story by introducing the main characters immediately.

How to do this:

- Reread page 1 with students. Right from the start, we sense the landlocked, hot place where red kangaroos live. Readers meet Big Red, who is licking his forearms as the evening breeze blows.
- On page 2, we see Red's ears twitch. He's surrounded by his mob and is alert to his surroundings. Readers can tell Red is always on guard in case there is danger nearby.

- Saxby's goal might have been to introduce Red to readers because we follow him throughout the rest of the book.
- Invite your small group to draft a lead that places their main character in a setting, doing something she or he typically does. Encourage them to give just enough information to get readers ready to interact with the main character throughout the rest of their writing.

Power Craft Move:	Precise Words
Name the craft:	Specific Nouns
Why authors do it:	Writers use specific nouns to help readers gain a deeper understanding of the characters and places featured in their books.
How to do this:	• Study two places in *Big Red Kangaroo* where specific nouns help readers understand who or what is doing the action. • On page 10, "Rainwater loiters in shallow pools, and Red drinks." The word *rainwater* lets readers know what remains on the ground for Red to drink. • On page 19, "The challenger retreats, all fight gone from him." The word *challenger* references the kangaroo who fought with the male for dominance of the mob. • You might choose to substitute less precise nouns or pronouns in the sentences so students can hear the difference between these words and the specific nouns. • Invite students to replace ambiguous nouns with specific ones in their drafts.

Power Craft Move:	Precise Words
Name the craft:	Vivid Verbs
Why authors do it:	Vivid verbs show readers precisely what is happening in a piece of writing.
How to do this:	• Study at least two of the following places in the text: • On page 6, "Red *flattens* his body, *extends* his tail, and *bounds* toward the trees, his mob close behind." The word *flattens* means levels, *extends* helps readers envision the way

Red elongates his tail to aid his balance, and *bounds* shows the way Red jumps through the air.

- Use this complex example with more sophisticated writers.
- On page 10, "Rainwater loiters in shallow pools, and Red drinks." The word *loiters* helps readers understand how the rainwater lingers on the ground.
- On page 20, "Red traverses the open plains with his mob." The word *traverses* helps readers understand the large area of land Red and the mob cross together.
- Debrief with students. Talk about the specificity of the words *bounds, extends, flattens, loiters,* and *traverses.* Help them think about how these words contrast with vague verbs.
- Invite students to replace vague verbs with stronger ones in their writing. Encourage them to choose verbs to help their readers envision the actions happening. Remind students to work toward drafting with stronger and more precise verbs going forward.

Power Craft Move: Punctuation to Create Voice

Name the craft: Hyphenated Words

Why authors do it: Writers sometimes use hyphens to join two or more words together to form a compound adjective.

How to do this:
- Study both of the following places in the text:
  - On page 1, "In the center of Australia, far inland, where ocean is a dim memory, the sun floats on the waves of another bake-earth day." The words *bake* and *earth* modify the word *day.* A single word could have been used to make *day* stand out, but Saxby choose to put two words together to help the reader understand how dry and hot it is on this day.
  - On page 20, "They will offer shade and shelter during the sizzle-bright day." The adjective *sizzle-bright* helps readers better comprehend how sunny and hot the day was.
  - For either of these sentences, you could demonstrate another way they could've been written without creating a compound adjective. Refer back to the way the compound adjective makes the sentence more vivid and precise if you do this.

- Invite students to create adjectives to enhance their writing voice by combining two words with a hyphen.

Power Craft Move: Teaching Tone

Name the craft: Clear Explanations

Why authors do it: Writers connect with readers by using a consistent tone in their writing. One way writers do this is by providing clear explanations of how things work so their readers can learn from their writing.

How to do this:
- Study two or more places in the text where Saxby crafts sentences that help the readers understand the information being provided in a clear way.
  - Reread page 3. Saxby defines the word *joey* by inserting the definition of the term in parentheses. Help students to understand the meaning of content-specific words so they will feel more at ease while reading the text.
  - Reread page 7. There's a clear explanation of how a kangaroo uses its tail (in case readers were confused by the description on page 6). By crafting three detailed sentences, Saxby helps readers understand the function of a red kangaroo's tail.
  - Reread page 11. Not only does Saxby explain what wallaroos, thorny devils, and spinifex are (referenced originally on page 10), but she also helps readers understand more about the way kangaroos stay hydrated. (This extra information, placed in italics on page 11, helps readers develop a greater understanding of the main text, in regular font.)
  - Reread page 13. Saxby explains how red kangaroos travel faster. Using "rather than" in the first sentence helps readers understand why longer hops are better than more hops.
- Invite students to use a teaching tone in their writing by providing a clear explanation of how things work for their readers. Encourage students to define content-specific vocabulary and explain complex information in a way that is easy to understand. Have students share what they drafted with someone who is unfamiliar with their text (specifically, not their writing partners) and ask that person whether what they've written is clear.

	# *Coral Reefs* by Seymour Simon
Publisher's Summary:	In *Coral Reefs,* Simon introduces elementary-school readers to the oceans' reefs through wonderful descriptions and stunning full-color photographs. He encourages appreciation of the ecology of coral reefs, explains why they are in danger, and suggests ways kids can help save the endangered reefs.
Power Craft Move:	Content-Specific Vocabulary
Name the craft:	Technical Language Teaches Readers About Topics
Why authors do it:	Nonfiction writers infuse their writing with technical language to teach their readers more about their topic. The technical language a writer chooses must be defined for readers. Writers often use commas to offset the definitions of words they define in context.
How to do this:	• Study at least two places in *Coral Reefs* where Simon embeds technical language and includes the definitions of those terms.

          • Note: Each of these words is defined more completely in the glossary on page 32. Simon does not italicize or use boldface for technical language.

          • Reread the sentence about the coral polyp on page 6. Think aloud about how embedding the definition in the sentence helps readers understand this technical language. An informal definition is included inside commas within the text, but a complete definition is in the glossary.

          • Reread the sentence about plankton on page 9. The word is defined early in the sentence so the technical word can come at the end. This helps readers understand the term's meaning.

                • Teach this only to students who aren't easily confused by learning two ways to do something in one lesson.

          • Reread the sentence about algae on page 9. The definition comes inside commas, just like the definition for *coral polyp.* Again, this is a more informal definition; a complete definition is in the glossary.

      • Invite students to include informal definitions for the technical language they want to use within the text, as Simon does. They can either insert commas around the definition or give the definition first and put the term at the end of the sentence (as in the *plankton* example).

Power Craft Move:	Ending

Name the craft: The Way We Are Known

Why authors do it: Writers often end their writing by focusing on the major accomplishments, qualities, or attributes of the person, object, or animal featured in their writing.

How to do this:
- Reread page 30 to your students. Simon contrasts architectural marvels to the way animals work together to build coral reefs. Draw students' attention to the colloquial phrase "out of this world" and talk about why this common phrase works here. Ask students to identify their lasting impressions of coral reefs based on the ending.
  - This ending speaks to the way we could know or remember coral. It starts out like a compare/contrast ending, but it feels more like the way Simon wants readers to understand the essence of a coral reef.
- Invite students to think of the most important thing about the subject of their writing. Ask them, "What is it known for?" Next, encourage students to do some jotting in their writer's notebook that they can use to create the final paragraph of their writing to emphasize what is most important about their subjects.

Power Craft Move:	Lead

Name the craft: Imagine Lead

Why authors do it: Narrative nonfiction writers can transport readers to other places by encouraging them to imagine something out of the ordinary. These leads are often written in the second person, inviting the reader to come along on a journey.

How to do this:
- Reread page 5 with your students. The first word is *Imagine*, which encourages the reader to think about something different. Simon draws readers into an underwater world. Words such as

you're and *you* make it seem as if Simon is talking directly to the reader.

- Invite your small group to draft an imagine lead. Encourage students to help readers consider a different life or a different place by starting off with "imagine . . ." or "what if . . ." (You might have students share the endings they write with other members of the group.)

Power Craft Move:	Precise Words
Name the craft:	Content-Specific Words
Why authors do it:	Writers find and use words that help their readers understand the topic. Often content-specific words are defined in context, in a sidebar, or in the book's glossary.
How to do this:	• Study two places in *Coral Reefs* where Simon embeds technical language and includes the definitions of those terms.

  - On page 14, barrier reefs are explained in the third paragraph. Ask students if they understand barrier reefs from the first sentence of the paragraph. Show students the definition of *barrier reef* in the glossary and explain how this helps readers who are unfamiliar with content-specific words.
  - On page 17, the word *anemone* appears in the first and third paragraphs. Start by showing students the definition of *anemone* in the glossary. Reread the third paragraph and look at the accompanying picture of the clownfish swimming among anemones. Talk to students about how photographs or drawings can enhance meaning when embedding content-specific words in the text.

- Invite students to use content-specific words to help readers understand the topic. Remind students to embed the definitions in the text or in a glossary. Encourage them to use drawings or photographs to beef up the meaning of content-specific words for readers, as Simon does on page 17.

Power Craft Move:	Precise Words
Name the craft:	Vivid Verbs

Why authors do it: Vivid verbs show readers precisely what is happening in a piece of writing.

How to do this:
- Study at least two of the following places in the text.
  - On page 6, "The polyp *buds* and *divides* again and again, developing into a large colony of thousands of mouths connected to one another." The words *buds* and *divides* show the reader how the polyp grows and separates to populate.
  - On page 6, "As nearby colonies *attach* to each other, the framework of a coral reef forms." The word *attach* helps readers envision colonies linking to one another to build something larger.
  - On page 17, "The reef *provides* shelter for thousands of fish species such as reef sharks, eels, parrotfish, angelfish, groupers, butterflyfish, pipefish, puffers, and rays." The word *provides* helps readers understand how the reef supplies shelter for so many fish.
  - Debrief with students. Talk about specific words like *buds, divides, attach,* and *provides.* Help them think about the precise nature of these words. If necessary, use nonexamples to help students hear the difference between vague verbs and precise ones.
- Invite students to find places in their writing in need of stronger verbs. Encourage them to find spots where they can strengthen the picture readers will make in their minds.

Power Craft Move: Punctuation to Create Voice

Name the craft: Hyphenated Words

Why authors do it: Writers sometimes use hyphens to join two or more words to form a compound adjective.

How to do this:
- Study at least two of the following places in the text.
  - On page 6, "Coral forms when a free-floating polyp attaches to a rock on a shallow seafloor of a tropical ocean." The words *free* and *floating* modify the word *polyp.* A single word might have been used to make the word *polyp* stand out, but instead Simon joined two words to modify it.

- On page 9, "Reef-building corals are called hard corals because their skeletons are made of limestone." The words *reef* and *building* are joined together with a hyphen so they can make the word corals more specific. The newly created word *reef-building* specifically describes the corals.
  - "Reef-building corals" is used again on page 10.
- On page 14, "Between fringing reefs and the shore are narrow, shallow-water places called lagoons." The word *shallow-water* modifies and describes *places*. The hyphenated adjective modifies the word *lagoons*.
- On page 18, "Colorful parrotfish use their chisel-like teeth to scrape coral for algae." The word *chisel-like* helps readers to understand how the parrotfish's teeth are sharp enough to scrape algae from the coral. Another possibility is to play with this sentence, showing how it might have been written without the compound adjective.
- Invite your students to give their writing voices greater precision by combining two or more words with a hyphen.

Power Craft Move: Text Features

Name the craft: Types of Print

Why authors do it: When writing an informational book, it's important to think about how to present information to readers. Writers and illustrators sometimes change the color of text when they want something to stand out on the page.

How to do this:
- Examine two pages in *Coral Reefs* where there's a different-color font. (Note: The text is indented. You might tuck that information into your explanations.)
  - On page 9, show readers how the words *table coral, branching coral,* and *brain coral* appear in blue. Talk about how this helps the information stand out. Correlate the terms to the three pictures that appear (left to right) on the bottom of the page.
  - On page 10, point out the words *sea fans, sea whips,* and *finger leather corals* that appear in blue. This time, ask your group how the blue makes the text stand out.

- These sentences not only alert readers to what's happening in the pictures, but they also are there in lieu of captions.
- Invite students to find some places where changing the color of their text could make information stand out. Like Simon, they might decide to change the color of text that describes an illustration. (Close by brainstorming other ways changing the color could help readers interact with their text.)

Power Craft Move:	Topics and Subtopics
Name the craft:	Grouping Related Information into Categories
Why authors do it:	One way many authors break up their topics is by linking related information. Writers divide their knowledge into categories even if they don't always include headings.
How to do this:	

- Study pages 10 and 18 with students. If a third example is needed, use the text on page 14.
  - Reread page 10 to students. Explain that this page of text (and the illustrations on page 11) focuses on the appearance of soft corals. Discuss why you think Simon devoted an entire page of text to this topic.
  - Reread page 14 to students. Ask, "What is this page mostly about?" If students have trouble answering, reread the first sentence on the page, which tells readers what that page of text is going to be about. (If your group is having trouble identifying the category each page is about, then provide one more example.)
  - Reread page 18 to students. This page is about the unique features of fish that live in coral reefs. Ask your students how they could figure that out since there's no introductory sentence on this page.
- Invite students to divide up the knowledge they have about their topics into different categories so they can teach readers about them. Like Simon, they can use introductory sentences (as on pages 10 and 14) to help readers understand what the information in a given section will be about.

Elizabeth, Queen of the Seas by Lynne Cox and Brian Floca

Publisher's Summary: Here is the incredible story of Elizabeth, a real-life elephant seal who made her home in the Avon River in the city of Christchurch, New Zealand. When Elizabeth decides to stretch out across a two-lane road, the citizens worry she might get hurt or cause traffic accidents, so a group of volunteers tows her out to sea. But Elizabeth swims all the way back to Christchurch. The volunteers catch her again and again—each time towing her farther, even hundreds of miles away— but Elizabeth still finds her way back home. Includes back matter with information about elephant seals.

Power Craft Move: Back Matter

Name the craft: Author's Note

Why authors do it: Some authors write narrative nonfiction—stories about real-life events. Sometimes the stories follow the exact sequence of events and sometimes they're embellished. Therefore, writers can include an author's note along with their text so readers can glean the facts about the text they're reading.

How to do this:
- Read the author's note on page 4 with your students. Talk about the backstory of *Elizabeth, Queen of the Seas* because the book seems unbelievable. However, Cox informs readers that Michael existed and that the story of Elizabeth is true.
- Invite students to separate fact from fiction in their text by writing an author's note. If the narrative nonfiction text seems unbelievable, encourage your students to craft an author's note to help readers understand that everything they're reading is the truth.

Power Craft Move: Back Matter

Name the craft: Fact Page

Why authors do it: Writers often share additional information to deepen readers' understanding of the text. Usually this is done on an additional page away from the main body of text.

How to do this:	• Reread page 45 with your students. The fact page includes information about elephant seals. Some of the information, such as Elizabeth's weight and appearance, is included in the text. However, not all the information on this final page would have fit into the story. Point out that information that does not help to build the world of the story should go on a page of its own.
	• Invite students to read through their note cards. Encourage them to look for interesting facts to enhance their readers' knowledge about their topic that might distract from the narrative nonfiction piece they're writing. Encourage them to create a fact page, as Cox does, that will deepen their readers' knowledge base or provide them with additional places, such as websites, where they can learn more.

Power Craft Move:	Ending
Name the craft:	Connecting with Readers
Why authors do it:	Writers want their stories to linger in the hearts and minds of readers long after they put down the text. This is an upbeat way to end a book because it connects readers to the story in a personal way.
How to do this:	• Reread pages 41–44 with your students. We can imagine how Elizabeth made her way back to the city of Christchurch. Highlight the second-to-last sentence of the book, on page 44, which repeats the first line of the lead. Explain how the repetition reinforces the central idea of this story. Draw attention to the final line of the book, also on page 44: "And that is exactly where she belonged." Explain to students how this final line draws you, as a reader, closer to the story, to the people of Christchurch, and to Elizabeth. Finally, discuss how this story will endure in your memory because of the ending.
	• Invite students whose narrative nonfiction texts finish on a positive note to try this kind of ending. Encourage them to connect with readers by trying out several lines that will linger in their hearts and minds. (You might have students share their endings with other members of the small group.)

Power Craft Move:	Lead

Name the craft: Meeting the Characters

Why authors do it: Even in nonfiction writing, authors bring readers into the world of the story by introducing the main characters immediately.

How to do this:
- Study pages 7–11 with your students. We're introduced to Elizabeth through description and illustrations on page 7. We're brought to where she has relocated—along the banks of the Avon River in Christchurch, New Zealand, which is a strange place to meet an elephant seal. On pages 8–9, we watch Elizabeth move out of the river and onto land to cool herself. We see how she's trying to adapt to her new surroundings in the city. On page 10 we learn some facts about Elizabeth, and we are introduced to her by her full name, "Elizabeth, Queen of the Seas," on page 11. Cox brings readers into Elizabeth's world to get a feeling of what her life is like.
- Invite your small group to draft a lead that places their main character in a setting and go about their typical actions. Encourage them to give readers just enough information to help them interact with the main character throughout the rest of their writing.

Power Craft Move:	Precise Words

Name the craft: Specific Nouns

Why authors do it: Writers use specific nouns to create solid sentences that help readers understand specific people, places, or things.

How to do this:
- Study at least two of the following places in the text.
  - On page 16, "The car hit a rock and dented its fender." The word *car* lets you know what screeched and banged into something.
  - On page 22, "Mother seals called to their babies with squeaks and squawks and whimpers, and babies squeaked back." This helps readers understand the sound the female adult seals made (in contrast to the sound adult males made in the previous sentence).

- On page 34, "Michael watched the water, and he wished upon the stars." On the previous page we learn that Michael and his friends were going about their normal lives. Yet the word *Michael* on this page lets us know exactly who was waiting and hoping that Elizabeth would come back.
- Talk about the specificity of these nouns. Some students might benefit from hearing you read each of the sentences, substituting vague nouns so they can hear the difference between imprecise and specific nouns.
- Invite students to replace ambiguous nouns with specific ones in their drafts.

Power Craft Move:	Precise Words
Name the craft:	Vivid Verbs
Why authors do it:	Vivid verbs show readers precisely what is happening in a piece of writing.
How to do this:	• Study at least two of the following places in the text.

- Study at least two of the following places in the text.
  - On page 15, "Early one morning, when the grass was still wet, Elizabeth hauled herself up, up, up to the top of the riverbank . . . and stretched out across the two-lane road." The word *hauled* helps readers picture the effort it took for a large elephant seal like Elizabeth to get out of the river and onto the road.
  - On page 31, "This time they towed Elizabeth to a seal colony, far, far away from the city." The word *towed* can help readers picture the way they led Elizabeth—who is massive—away from Christchurch.
  - On page 38, "Michael ran to tell his friends, who told their families, who all came down to the spot on the bridge." The word *ran* shows readers how excited Michael was when Elizabeth returned to the city.
  - Debrief with students. Talk about the specificity of the words *hauled*, *towed*, and *ran*. Help students think about the way these verbs show precise movement.
- Invite students to find places in their writing in need of stronger verbs. Encourage them to look for spots where they want to strengthen the picture readers will make in their minds.

Power Craft Move:	Punctuation to Create Voice
Name the craft:	Dashes
Why authors do it:	Writers use dashes to emphasize, interrupt, or change a thought in a sentence. The sentence will still make sense if the words in between the dashes are removed. Dashes can also substitute for parentheses.

How to do this:	• Study the following places in the text.
	  • On page 10, "She was eight feet long—as long as a long surfboard—and she weighed twelve hundred pounds—as much as fifteen Labrador retrievers." The information gives readers a better sense of Elizabeth's size because it compares her to things readers might comprehend. The comparisons also give readers a more concrete way to picture Elizabeth.
	  • On page 12, "Though Michael knew never to get too close to her—after all, she was a wild animal—he liked to call out her name." The information inside the dashes helps readers understand *why* Michael didn't get too close to Elizabeth. Discuss how the sentence would still be complete without the information between the dashes, but the inclusion emphasizes what Michael knows about elephant seals.
	  • Note: Both of the examples from the text show emphasis.
	• Invite students to enhance their texts by placing information between dashes to emphasize, interrupt, or change a thought. Students who have written their texts with information in parentheses might try replacing them with dashes.

Power Craft Move:	Repetition
Name the craft:	Repetition of Words, Phrases, and Actions
Why authors do it:	Writers intentionally repeat words or phrases to create a mood for readers.
How to do this:	• Cox uses repetition in four distinct ways in this text. Study one or more of the ways, depending on the group of students with whom you're working.

- Repetition of the word *maybe* appears several times in the text. You might surmise that Cox uses this to explain Elizabeth's motivation. On pages 15 and 24, for example, she employs the word *maybe*.
- Repetition of a single word for emphasis. On page 15, the word *up* is repeated three times. On page 31, the word *far* is repeated twice.
  - On page 41, the word *must* is repeated in three different sentences. This example is different than the other two single-word examples, so include it only if you think it will help your students.
- Repetition of an action. On pages 14, 28, and 36, Elizabeth snorts once to clear the water from her nostrils and again as if she is saying hello. (The reason for the initial snort is explained on page 14.) Speak about the way this repeated action ties the story together or fosters an emotional connection.
- Repetition of the first words in a sentence. On page 32, two sentences begin with the words "Each day." The third sentence on the page begins with "But then one day." Talk about the rhythm this pattern creates for readers.
- Invite students to try at least one type of repetition in their writing. Encourage them to be intentional about the placement of the repetition so it creates a desired effect for readers.

Power Craft Move: Text Features

Name the craft: Maps and Pictures

Why authors do it: Writers include text features like maps and pictures to deepen their readers' understanding of a nonfiction text.

How to do this:
- Examine page 4 with students. Remind them that maps help readers to understand where things are located in the world. The map on this page helps readers to understand that Christchurch is in the southern part of New Zealand, surrounded by the Pacific Ocean.
- Look at page 10 with your students. Point out the New Zealand stamp and mention that the country is part of the British

monarchy. (Note: "New Zealand is a constitutional monarchy with The Queen as Sovereign" [http://www.royal.gov.uk/monarchandcommonwealth/newzealand/thequeensrolein-newzealand.aspx].) This stamp helps readers understand why the elephant seal was named after Queen Elizabeth II.

- Invite students to create text features to enhance meaning for their readers. Students can pull their note cards to see what might be better represented as a text feature, or they can scan their drafts, circle a place where a text feature would be useful to readers, and then create that text feature.

| **Power Craft Move:** | Text Features |

Name the craft: Types of Print

Why authors do it: When writing an informational book, it's important to think about how to present information to readers. One thing writers and illustrators do is change the font when they want something to stand out on the page.

How to do this:
- Examine some of the following pages that feature different fonts.
  - On page 11, point out how the name Elizabeth, Queen of the Seas is written in a larger, cursive font, which suggests the regal connection to the seal's namesake.
  - On page 13, Michael's words are written in a large cursive font. His words do not have quotation marks around them. Rather, they're inside a speech bubble.
  - On page 16, the word *bang* is written in all caps and in a larger, italicized font. This makes the action of the car hitting the rock stand out for the reader (beyond what the illustration does).
  - On page 28 and 36, Michael's words are written in large, cursive font. Again, there are no dialogue tags. (You may choose to point out that his words aren't always written out like this. See page 21.)
  - On pages 38 and 39, the words the people of Christchurch said are written without dialogue tags, in large, cursive font. You might point out the similarity to Michael's spoken words on pages 13 and 28.
- Invite students to find places in their writing where changing the font can make information stand out.

Founding Mothers: Remembering the Ladies by Cokie Roberts and Diane Goode

Publisher's Summary:	Beautifully illustrated by Caldecott Honor–winning artist Diane Goode, *Founding Mothers: Remembering the Ladies* reveals the incredible accomplishments of the women who orchestrated the American Revolution behind the scenes. Roberts traces the stories of heroic, patriotic women such as Abigail Adams, Martha Washington, Phillis Wheatley, Mercy Otis Warren, Sarah Livingston Jay, and others. Details are gleaned from their letters, private journals, lists, and ledgers. The bravery of these women's courageous acts contributed to the founding of America and spurred the founding fathers to make this a country that "remembered the ladies."

This compelling book supports the Common Core State Standards with a rich time line, biographies, an author's note, and additional web resources in the back matter. |

Power Craft Move:	Content-Specific Vocabulary
Name the craft:	Defining Words in Context
Why authors do it:	Nonfiction writers infuse their writing with technical language to teach their readers more about a topic. Writers must define technical language so readers can understand the content. Writers can use dashes to offset the definitions of words they define in context.

How to do this:	• Study at least two places in *Founding Mothers* where Roberts uses dashes to offset the definitions of words. Two possibilities:
	  • Reread page 10. In order to explain what farms in the South were called, Roberts uses the word *plantations*. Roberts probably knows some of her readers won't know the term, so she defines them as "big farms" inside dashes. Teach students that once they define a word, they may use it repeatedly without redefining it in the text.
	  • Reread the sentence containing the word *patriots* on page 14. Show students how Roberts again sets off the definition inside dashes. Explain how the definition helps readers understand the rest of the sentence. Point out that Roberts's consistent style helps readers know when a content-specific word is being defined.

- Invite students to use technical language to teach their readers about a topic. Encourage students to consistently define technical terms in context, using dashes.

Power Craft Move:	Lead

Name the craft: Letter to the Reader

Why authors do it: Nonfiction writers craft introductions to get their readers ready to interact with their material. Sometimes they speak directly to their readers by writing them a letter.

How to do this:
- Study the letter of introduction on pages 6 and 7. It acknowledges the reader as a friend on page 6 and is signed by the author at the bottom of page 7. Mention how Roberts's interest in history led to her career in politics and eventually to this book. Make note of the third paragraph where Roberts references the primary sources she uncovered while researching this book. This highlights how Roberts spent lots of time researching the information in this book. The fourth paragraph helps readers to understand Roberts's purpose for writing the book—she believes women and men were equally important to the nation's founding. In total, the letter of introduction establishes Roberts's passion and purpose for the book she has written while addressing the reader in a friendly way.
- Invite students to craft a letter of introduction for their writing.

Power Craft Move:	Precise Words

Name the craft: Specific Nouns

Why authors do it: Writers select strong, specific nouns to add power to their sentences.

How to do this:
- Study at least two places in the text where the author used specific nouns. Some examples:
  - On page 14, "So politicians depended on newspapers and pamphlets to spread their messages." Replace the word *politicians* with *people* and reread the sentence. Then, talk about the specificity of the word *politicians,* which refers to those who used newspapers and pamphlets to learn about the news.

- On page 27, "General Washington demanded the women use the cash to buy linen for shirts." Show students that the word *he* can't be substituted because this is the first mention of Washington. Point out how using the word *General* makes it even clearer to readers that Roberts is referring to General George Washington.
- On page 28, "When the Jays returned to America with their two little girls born abroad, it was the first time Sally had seen her little boy in five years." Start out by noting how *the Jays* provides more specific information than the pronoun *they*. Likewise, the name *Sally* is more specific than *she* (even though readers can infer that Roberts is talking about Sarah Livingston).
- Invite students to replace vague nouns with specific ones. Remind them of the importance of drafting with specific nouns going forward.

Power Craft Move:	Precise Words

Name the craft: Vivid Verbs

Why authors do it: Selecting the right words is as important when writing nonfiction as when writing fictional narratives. Interesting words are one of the marks of strong informational writing. Verbs can be the most significant part of a sentence because they show what is happening.

How to do this:
- Study at least two places in the text where the author uses vivid verbs. Here are three possibilities:
  - On page 11, Roberts uses the verb *cultivated*. Reread the sentence where the word appears and explain what it means. The word *cultivated* works because it creates a more active picture in readers' minds.
  - On page 18, she uses the verb *printed*. Reread the sentence where it appears. Explain how you get a clearer picture in your mind with the word *printed*.
  - On page 23, Roberts uses the verb *directed*. Reread the sentence where it appears and explain what it means in this context. Try replacing *directed* with *told* to show students how the former is a stronger choice. Surmise that Roberts chose the word *directed* because Martha was giving orders to the slaves.

- Invite students to edit their writing. Encourage them to use verbs that will help their writing come to life.
  - Although we want students to stretch their vocabularies, we don't want their writing to be littered with words they cannot pronounce or understand. If you encourage your students to use a thesaurus, make sure they reread their new sentences aloud to ensure the new verbs make sense.

Power Craft Move:	Punctuation to Create Voice
Name the craft:	Parenthetical References
Why authors do it:	Sometimes authors add parentheses to clarify something for readers or to make writing sound more conversational.
How to do this:	• Study two places in *Founding Mothers* where Roberts includes information in parentheses, which provides a conversational tone.

- Study two places in *Founding Mothers* where Roberts includes information in parentheses, which provides a conversational tone.
  - On page 16, Roberts uses parentheses twice.
    - Reread the introductory paragraph. Alter your voice when you read the text in parentheses. Talk about how the text in the parentheses makes it feel as if Roberts is speaking directly to readers and sharing a secret.
    - Reread the paragraph beneath the "Letters" subheading. Change the tone of your voice when you're reading the text in the parentheses. Surmise that Roberts wants readers to know that it's okay to read letters written by people long deceased.
  - On page 30, Roberts includes parenthetical references in the second and third paragraphs. Because the parenthetical reference in the second paragraph is similar to the ones on page 16, I recommend sharing that one only.
    - Reread the second paragraph. Change your tone again when you share the secret contained inside the parentheses. Point out how the information in the parentheses helps us understand Catherine Littlefield. Roberts might have included the information about women not wearing pants back then to show how Littlefield strayed from social conventions.
  - It is important to show students how few parenthetical references there are in *Founding Mothers* so their writing doesn't become riddled with parentheses.

- Invite students to insert parentheses sparingly into their writing. Remind them they can include information in parentheses anytime they want to get more conversational with their reader, as Roberts does in *Founding Mothers*.

Power Craft Move: Quotes and Sources

Name the craft: Partial Quotes

Why authors do it: Writers use quotation marks to set off the real words people say. Sometimes writers quote only part of what a person says.

How to do this:
- Study three places in the text with students:
  - Reread the following sentence on page 12: "Deborah was left to run everything, and Ben thought she did an excellent job of managing money, saying she was 'a fortune' to him."
    - Point out that Roberts puts quotations around just two words in the sentence. Discuss the importance of using transitions to frame the full quote, which enables writers to quote only what's necessary for understanding.
  - Reread the last paragraph on page 15.
    - Point out how the final sentence in the paragraph helps us understand that all the quotations are taken from the writing of Mercy Otis Warren. Then, explain how partial quotations can be used when we excerpt something from a person's writing, not just when we attribute speech. Make note of how Roberts uses five sets of quotation marks within two sentences in that paragraph, providing readers with the context, rather than dumping in long lines from Mercy Otis Warren's writing about General Washington and General Lee.
  - Reread the "Remember the Ladies" paragraph on page 16.
    - Have a printout of the full text of Adams's quote, from http://www.history.com/this-day-in-history/abigail-adams-urges-husband-to-remember-the-ladies, beside you. Compare and contrast the lengthy and partial quotes. Talk with students about how readers can better understand what Adams meant without using so much text. Talk with students about the process Roberts may have gone

through to select the right words from the original quotation to share with readers of *Founding Mothers*.

- Invite students to pare down some of their quotations by selecting key words from important quotations. Remind them to carefully select the words they're going to quote so the quote doesn't lose its meaning for readers. Have students check in with you after they write one or two partial quotes to ensure that they're providing meaningful transitions and context.

Power Craft Move:	Teaching Tone
Name the craft:	Talking to the Audience
Why authors do it:	Writers connect with readers by using a consistent tone in their writing. One of the ways writers do this is by using phrases to explain their thinking and engage with their audience.
How to do this:	

- Study at least two places in the text where Roberts talks directly to the reader.
    - On page 16, reread the entire "Letters" paragraph. Roberts addresses readers directly by using the word *you* in the second sentence. Make note of the text in the parentheses, which is like sharing a tip with readers. Talk about the way Roberts shares her emotions in the final line of the paragraph, "Thank goodness we have the ones we do!"
    - On page 19, "It might surprise you that Phillis Wheatley lived in Boston, since we think of slavery as Southern." After you reread this sentence, point to the word *you* so students understand that talking to readers directly engages them. Suggest that one's interaction with the text and subject matter would have changed if the sentence had just read: "Phillis Wheatley lived in Boston." Roberts talks to readers and anticipates their surprise at discovering that slavery existed outside the South.
    - On page 20, reread the entire paragraph with an emphasis on the final sentence, "Think how alone she must have felt!" Suggest that Roberts engages readers with this line because she has just been discussing all the things Abigail Adams endured while her husband was away. It's as if Roberts is saying *you need to think about this, reader!* Point out that

> Roberts is still talking directly to readers, although *you* is implied in the sentence.

- Invite students to talk directly to their audience in their writing. For inexperienced and some mid-range writers, using *you* directly might be the best choice. Other mid-range and sophisticated writers might craft short phrases that imply *you*. Although we want to encourage students to engage with their readers, we must remind them to do this sparingly (as Roberts does) so they maintain a tone that teaches readers rather than one that feels too conversational.

Power Craft Move:	Text Features
Name the craft:	Print Layout
Why authors do it:	When writing an informational book, it's important to think about how to present information to readers, including the page layout.
How to do this:	• Examine page spreads in the book that contain interesting layouts. Two possibilities:

- Examine page spreads in the book that contain interesting layouts. Two possibilities:
  - On the page spread (18–19) about Phillis Wheatley, the verso, or left, page is laid out like the rest of biographical profiles of the other founding mothers. Show students how the recto, or right, page contains one of Wheatley's poems. Hypothesize about why Roberts choose to embed one of Wheatley's poems on this page.
  - On the page spread (24–25) about Women Warriors, point out that there are two introductory paragraphs underneath the heading. Show students how each of the five subheadings and facts support the big topic. Talk about why this page spread includes subheadings and how this helps readers understand more about the big idea of women as warriors.
- Invite students to plan the layout of the pages in their informational books. A few pages could be laid out in a unique way to support the text.
  - Encourage students to pick a page that could benefit from a unique layout, like the ones they studied in *Founding Mothers*.

Power Craft Move:	Text Features

Name the craft: Time Lines

Why authors do it: Writers use time lines to show past events in chronological order. Time lines help readers understand when specific events happened.

How to do this:
- Study the time line on pages 8 and 9.
  - Point out that the time line is located in the front of the book. We get a preview of significant women in the book by encountering them first through this time line. The time line's title is "Women Through the Years" and it spans fifty years. Remark on how almost every item on the time line helps readers understand what was happening in history during a particular year *and* how it affected women.
- Invite students to select important events for their time lines. Encourage them to write one or two sentences, as Roberts does, to explain each dot on their time line.

Power Craft Move:	Topics and Subtopics

Name the craft: Grouping Related Information and Illustrations

Why authors do it: Nonfiction writers teach readers about a big topic. Writers (and illustrators) create categories by grouping related information and illustrations when they're writing an informational book.

How to do this:
- Study at least two places in *Founding Mothers* where Roberts and Goode group related information and illustrations together. These appear on the pages that portray women writers and women warriors through prose and pictures.
  - The header on pages 16–17 says "Women Writers." The header gets you ready to read about female writers during the Revolutionary Era. All of the subheadings, paragraphs, and illustrations support the idea that women wrote during this time period. Hypothesize that the subtopic of women as writers emerged because Roberts uses a variety of primary sources, many of them written by women.
  - The header on pages 24–25 says "Women Warriors." Readers expect to learn about women who fought in the

Revolutionary War. Scan the page spread and talk about the subheadings and how they are related to the bigger idea. Talk about how the illustrations refer back to the topic of the page spread. Summarize by stating that all the writing and illustrations support the big idea of this page, which is that women were involved in various aspects of the Revolutionary War.

- Invite students to narrow the information they've collected. Have them divide their knowledge into different subtopics or categories and then group related information and drawings as they write their information books.

I See a Pattern Here by Bruce Goldstone

Publisher's Summary:	Patterns are fascinating! They can be so beautiful that people come from all over the world to see them, or so familiar you hardly notice them. They appear everywhere: beehives, dinner plates, even the bottoms of your shoes! With stunning photographs that show diverse examples from nature and artwork around the world, Bruce Goldstone reveals the secrets behind patterns—and gives you some fun ideas for making your own.
Power Craft Move:	Back Matter
Name the craft:	Information Page
Why authors do it:	Writers often include an informational page at the end of their text so readers can further immerse themselves in the topic.
How to do this:	• Study pages 30–31 with students. Make note of the heading and subheadings. These are the author's way of helping readers make meaning by providing several project ideas to help them learn more about patterns. Point out technical language such as *flips, slides,* and *turns* that Goldstone embeds in the text. Discuss how embedding these terms lets readers practice using the vocabulary as they engage in the activities. • Invite students to create a project-based information page that will follow the conclusion of their nonfiction writing. Encourage them to create activities for their readers that will extend their knowledge about the topic.

| **Power Craft Move:** | Content-Specific Vocabulary |

| **Name the craft:** | Technical Language Teaches Readers About Topics |

| **Why authors do it:** | Nonfiction writers infuse their writing with technical language to teach their readers more about their topic. The technical language must be defined for readers. Writers can define words in context or use text features that include the definitions. |

How to do this:

- Study two places in *I See a Pattern Here* where Goldstone defines technical language in speech balloons, which he calls "MathSpeak."
  - Reread the MathSpeak balloon on page 6. In order to explain how *slide* means the same thing as *translation,* Goldstone states that "a translation is a move from one place to another." The picture of the seals on page 6 shows how it can be moved in any direction to make a pattern. Point out other slide/translation examples in the brick pattern on page 7 and the fence pattern on page 9.
  - Reread the MathSpeak balloon on page 20. Goldstone explains *scaling* as "changing the size of a shape" by making it bigger or smaller. He also uses words such as *increase* and *decrease* to explain further how scaling works. Readers need to understand what scaling means in order to understand the examples on pages 20–23. As with all the pattern concepts in this book, Goldstone explicitly defines the technical language so readers will have a better understanding of the terminology.
- Invite students to create speech balloons that will define the technical language they're embedding in their writing. Encourage them to boldface the words they're defining in speech balloons, as Goldsteone does, so those words will stand out for readers. You might ask students to explain the function of their speech balloons, as Goldstone does on page 3.
  - Note: There's also a text features craft lesson for this book on how to teach writers to embed speech balloons in their writing.

| **Power Craft Move:** | Ending |

| **Name the craft:** | Summary List |

Why authors do it: Writers recap the main ideas to remind readers of all the things they learned from a text.

How to do this:
- Reread pages 28–29 to your students. The final spread sums up everything readers learned about flips, scaling, slides, symmetry, tiling, and turns. The two-page mosaic pattern includes all the patterns, which encourages readers to use their newfound knowledge. Page 28 includes two questions that invite readers to use their knowledge of patterns to engage with the illustration.
  - The ending of this book is almost like an invitation for readers to try out what they've learned.
- Invite students to write a summary list ending. Encourage them to touch on each of their big topics in their writing, pulling together everything they taught their readers into a cohesive ending.

Power Craft Move: Lead

Name the craft: Definition Lead

Why authors do it: Writers use definitions at the beginning of texts to alert readers about important terminology and build their schema, which allows them to interact with the text that follows.

How to do this:
- Reread page 2. Point out the first sentence, which includes a basic definition of pattern. The next few sentences help readers understand how often a pattern may repeat (i.e., once, many times, forever). Study the illustrations, which are graphic examples of patterns. The illustrations on pages 2 and 3 show readers a variety of patterns, which gets them ready for the information Goldstone presents in the book.
- Invite students to define one or two crucial terms for readers and include these in the lead paragraph of their texts. Encourage students to select one or two words that will help their readers understand the terminology and provide a base for understanding the topic of their writing.

Power Craft Move: Teaching Tone

Name the craft: Talking to the Audience

Why authors do it: Writers connect with readers by using a consistent tone. One way they do this is by adopting a conversational voice.

How to do this:
- Study two places in the text where Goldstone talks directly to readers.
  - On page 14, Goldstone explains *flipping* by providing a concrete explanation and thorough pictures. He gets readers to imagine they're doing the flip. Point out the use of the second-person pronouns.
  - On page 25, note the way Goldstone writes in the second person, employing the word *you* three times on this page. Talk about how this technique engages the reader.
- Invite students to talk directly to their readers by crafting sentences that speak to their audience in key places in their text.

Power Craft Move: Text Features

Name the craft: Captions

Why authors do it: Writers use captions to help readers understand pictures or photographs.

How to do this:
- Study two places where Goldstone writes sentences to tell more about the illustration:
  - On page 23, Goldstone writes two to three sentences to explain each image. Hypothesize that he must have written longer captions because the concept of scaling might be difficult for readers to understand. Each caption explains the picture.
  - On page 27, Goldstone crafts three captions to describe the tessellations in the images. Ask students, "Why do you think Goldstone writes so much about each of these pictures?" Have students consider how each caption contributes to a reader's understanding of the picture.
- Invite students to write captions for drawings or images they include in their nonfiction writing. Encourage them to craft a couple of sentences, rather than just a few words, to help readers deepen their meaning of the content by reading the caption and looking at the illustration.

Power Craft Move:	Text Features

Name the craft:	Headings

Why authors do it: Nonfiction writers use headings to introduce their categories to readers. By naming a category with a heading, writers are telling their readers what the words and drawings on the page will mostly be about. The heading is like the main idea, and everything that follows is supporting information.

How to do this:
- Examine two page spreads in the text that contain headings:
  - On page 6, the heading says "Ride the Slide." Think aloud to show students what you'd expect to learn on pages 6–9, which fall under the same heading. Reference the MathSpeak bubble to show how you're using all the information on the page to think about the text. If necessary, reread the text and examine the illustrations to determine if you learn something about slides, or translations, on these pages. Note how writing and illustrations work together to teach us about the main idea contained in the heading.
  - On page 24, the heading says "Color Counts." This time, invite students to state what they expect to learn from these pages. Ask them, "are all the text and illustrations about color on this page?" Elicit evidence from your students.
  - Point out that each heading is a short phrase or sentence. For sophisticated writers, you can make a note of the alliteration, rhyme, and punchy phrases and questions Goldstone crafts as headings.
- Invite students to write the headings for each category of their informational books. As Goldstone did, they can craft headings that are catchy short phrases.

Power Craft Move:	Text Features

Name the craft:	Print Layout

Why authors do it: When writing an informational book, it's important to think about how to present information to readers. One thing that writers and illustrators think about is the way they'll lay out information on each page.

How to do this:
- Examine three page spreads in the book that contain interesting layouts. Some possibilities:
  - On the "Flipping Out" page spread (14–15), the verso page has a line of reflection drawn down the center. It's a concrete example of a flip. Note the way arrows are used to draw readers' attention to specific pictures on pages 14 and 15. Show students how the writing is contained in the illustration on page 15. Arrows focus readers' attention (because the illustration is of a picture frame) by pointing toward the illustrations.
  - On the "Follow the Fold" page spread (18–19), the verso page is laid out like most of the other introductory pages to each topic. The recto page has items dispersed around the page. The text moves toward the center of the page and encourages readers to find the lines of symmetry. Ask students: "Why do you think Goldstone put the text toward the center of the page rather than on the top or the bottom?" and "What kind of effect does the text in the middle of the page have for you as a reader?"
  - On page 21, there are two images on the page, but only one caption. The caption is to the right of the image it refers to, which makes it easy for readers to know which picture is being described.
- Invite students to plan the layout of the pages in their informational books. Stress a consistent look, but a few pages could be laid out in a way that will support the writing.
  - Encourage students to pick a page from their own writing that could benefit from a unique layout, like the ones you studied in *I See a Pattern Here*.

Power Craft Move:　Text Features

Name the craft:　Speech Balloons

Why authors do it:　Nonfiction writers infuse their writing with technical language to teach their readers more about topics. The technical language must be defined for readers.

How to do this:
- Study three places in *I See a Pattern Here* where Goldstone defines technical language in the MathSpeak speech balloons.

- Reread the MathSpeak balloon on page 10. Notice there are two words being equated: *turn* and *rotation*. Point out the boldface print for both terms in the balloon: *rotation* and *point of rotation*. Discuss how this definition makes it easier to understand the concept of rotation on pages 10–13.
- Reread the MathSpeak balloon on page 12. Although Goldstone could have used the words *upside-down turns* at the top of page 12, he wanted to teach readers the technical term, *180-degree turn,* for this concept.
- Reread the MathSpeak balloon on page 26. Goldstone equates *tile pattern* with *tessellation,* which he defines in the speech balloon. Note the boldface definition in the balloon. Defining *tessellation* helps readers understand all the patterns on pages 26 and 27 as examples.
- Invite students to create speech balloons to define content-specific words. Encourage them to boldface the words they're defining to ensure that readers will notice.

Power Craft Move: Text Features

Name the craft: Types of Print

Why authors do it: When writing an informational book, it's important to think about how to present information to readers. Writers use a variety of fonts to show readers what is important to know.

How to do this:
- Study two places in the text where Goldstone uses boldface font treatment.
  - On page 18, show readers that the words *symmetry* and *line of symmetry* are in boldface. Talk about how this helps readers notice the information. Correlate to the pictures of the frog and the letters spelling the word *match* that have lines of symmetry running through them.
  - On page 29, point out the words *transform* and *transformations,* which appear in boldface. Ask your group, "How does the boldface make the text stand out?" These sentences not only alert readers to changes in the patterns, but they also define content-specific words.
- Invite students to find some places where changing the font treatment can make information stand out.

Power Craft Move: Topics and Subtopics

Name the craft: Grouping Related Information into Categories

Why authors do it: One way many authors break up their topics is by categorizing related information.

How to do this:
- Headings are Goldstone's way of clustering related information into categories. Study three places in the text where Goldstone groups related information:
  - Study pages 10–13 with students. Explain that these pages deal with turns, or rotation. The first paragraph on page 10 tells more about the topic. A speech balloon defines *turn* on page 10. Show students the examples of turns found on pages 11–13. All the information on these four pages is related to turns.
  - Study pages 18–21 with students. Ask, "What is this page mostly about?" If students have trouble answering, reread the first paragraph on page 18 and the speech balloon definitions. Discuss how the information on pages 19–21 relates to the information on page 18.
- Invite students to divide the knowledge about their topics into categories that will help to teach readers about their big idea. As Goldstone does, they can use a few sentences to introduce each topic. (Some writers may choose to use headings to break their writing into categories. Note the text features craft lesson about how to teach writers to craft headings in their writing on page 175.)

No Monkeys, No Chocolate by Melissa Stewart, Allen Young, and Nicole Wong

Publisher's Summary: This delectable dessert comes from cocoa beans, which grow on cocoa trees in tropical rain forests. But those trees couldn't survive without the help of a menagerie of rain forest critters: a pollen-sucking midge, an aphid-munching anole lizard, brain-eating coffin fly maggots—they all pitch in to help the cocoa tree survive. A secondary layer of text delves deeper into statements such as "Cocoa flowers can't bloom without cocoa leaves . . . and maggots," explaining the interdependence of the plants and animals in the tropical rain forests. Two wise-cracking bookworms appear on every page, adding humor and further commentary, making this book accessible to readers of different ages and reading levels.

Back matter includes information about cocoa farming and rain forest preservation, as well as an author's note.

Power Craft Move:	Back Matter
Name the craft:	Fact Page
Why authors do it:	Authors present factual information that doesn't fit into the central story in a separate section of their book called the back matter.
How to do this:	• Reread the headings atop each page to refresh students' memories about the "story" in *No Monkeys, No Chocolate*. Then read page 30, "Cocoa and Rain Forests." The facts on this page are presented in a more traditional format, including expository paragraphs and no additional illustrations.

- Highlight two facts mentioned on this page that don't fit into the secondary text, or the details, of the book.
  - On traditional cocoa farms, workers plant cocoa trees in neat rows with only a few kinds of trees shading them from the sun.
  - In the last thirty years, more than 40 percent of the world's tropical rain forests have been destroyed.
  - Explain that Stewart and Young must have thought this information was important to include for readers, even though it doesn't fit into the "story."
- Invite students to examine their note cards for interesting facts that don't fit with the main body of their writing. Have them create fact pages similar to the one in *No Monkeys, No Chocolate*.

Power Craft Move:	Back Matter
Name the craft:	Call to Action Page
Why authors do it:	Authors anticipate their writing will make their audience care about an issue. Writers compose a list of suggestions to help their readers take action.

How to do this: • Study the "What You Can Do to Help" page in the back matter.
- • Stewart and Young suspect their readers will care about rain forest preservation after reading their book. Highlight the first, second, and third items on the list, which provide readers with ways they can help to protect and preserve rain forests.
- • The bulleted list under the fourth item provides readers with simple ways they can reduce their impact on Earth.
- • Invite students to think of ways their readers might take action as a result of reading their writing. Encourage students to be proactive by anticipating ways their audience might want to make a difference. Then, have them go back to their focus spots to create a "call to action" page where they recommend things readers can do to bring about change or learn more about the topic.

Power Craft Move: Content-Specific Vocabulary

Name the craft: Technical Language That Teaches Readers About Topics

Why authors do it: Nonfiction writers infuse their writing with technical language to teach their readers more about their topic. The technical language must be defined.

How to do this: • Study one or both of the following places in *No Monkeys, No Chocolate* where Stewart and Young embed technical language.
- • Reread the paragraph that starts with "Aphids" on page 20. Focus on the first sentence, which provides readers with an understanding of what aphids do. It begins with the term and then defines it for readers. In addition, the entire paragraph helps readers understand what aphids do.
- • Reread the first paragraph about hyphae on page 24. The definition comes prior to the term's being defined. As readers continue reading on page 24, *hyphae* is used two more times, which assumes readers now understand the term's meaning.
  - • Teach this defining technique to sophisticated readers so they'll be able to use it.
- • Invite students to write informal definitions within the text for the technical language they want to include in their texts, as Stewart and Young do. They can either embed the definitions in a sen-

tence following the word (by using the word *is* or *are*) or state the definition first and follow with the term (like the *hyphae* example).

Power Craft Move:	Ending

Name the craft: Circular Ending

Why authors do it: In fiction, a circular ending returns to the beginning arc of the story. Writers can also use this technique in narrative nonfiction.

How to do this:
- Reread pages 3–5, where readers learn that you must have cocoa beans to make chocolate. Next, jump to page 26, which is where the cocoa bean is mentioned again. This time, readers learn that a new tree will grow if the cocoa bean "lands in just the right place." On the final page spread of the book, 28–29, we learn that monkeys are the ones that scatter the cocoa beans to the ground, which is what allows the beans to root in the ground and sprout new trees. This circular approach begins and ends with cocoa beans.
  - Make note of the bookworm on page 29 that says, "That's right, no monkeys, no chocolate. The seeds monkeys spit out end up growing into new trees." This will reinforce the point about the cocoa beans being seeds, which grow into new trees.
- Invite students to craft a circular ending. Encourage them to review the beginning of their writing. Writers ask themselves, "Can I have my writing end in the same place, making something come full circle, as Stewart and Young do?"

Power Craft Move:	Lead

Name the craft: Asking a Question

Why authors do it: Nonfiction authors commonly open their writing with questions that will immediately engage readers.

How to do this:
- Reread page 4 with your students. Emphasize the question on the fourth line. Point out how the authors answer their question with their opinions. Make note of the sensory details that precede the question, which prompts readers to agree that chocolate is what makes the desserts delicious.

- Invite students to draft a lead that asks a question. Encourage them to provide readers with relevant information before the question (as Stewart and Young do) to engage readers.

Power Craft Move:	Precise Words

Name the craft: Specific Nouns

Why authors do it: Writers use specific nouns to help readers understand people, places, or things.

How to do this:
- Study two places in *No Monkeys, No Chocolate*:
  - On page 10, "Pollen travels down the tube." The word *pollen* lets you know what is moving down the tube inside the blossom.
  - On page 16, "As soon as leaf-cutter ants spot tender, new leaves on a cocoa tree, the little insects race to reach them." Using the word *leaf-cutter* prior to *ants* provides clarifying information that helps readers understand that the ants cut and carry pieces of leaves.
  - Some students might benefit from hearing you read each of the sentences with less precise nouns or pronouns as substitutes.
- Invite students to replace ambiguous nouns with specific ones in their writing.

Power Craft Move:	Precise Words

Name the craft: Vivid Verbs

Why authors do it: Vivid verbs show readers precisely what is happening in a piece of writing.

How to do this:
- Study at least two of the following places in the text.
  - On page 16, "When the eggs hatch, tiny maggots *wriggle* out and eat the ants' brains." The word *wriggle* shows readers how maggots twist and turn their bodies to move.
  - On page 20, "The little lizard *skitters* along the tree's branches, eating aphids and other insects" The word *skitters* helps readers picture the lizard running quickly on the branches.

- On page 28, "Monkeys *yank* pods off cocoa trees, *gnaw* holes in the fruits, and *pull* out the sticky insides." The verbs in this sentence help readers envision exactly how the monkeys grab, bite on, and reach into the cocoa pods.
- Debrief with students. Discuss how specific verbs such as *gnaw, pull, skitters, wriggle,* and *yank* powerfully describe the ants' actions. Use nonexamples to help students hear the difference between a vague action verb and a precise one.
- Invite students to find places in their writing in need of stronger verbs. Encourage them to look for spots where they want to strengthen the picture readers will make in their minds.

Power Craft Move:	Teaching Tone

Name the craft: Clear Explanations

Why authors do it: Writers connect with their readers by using a consistent tone in their writing. One way writers do this is by providing clear explanations of how things work.

How to do this:
- Study two places in the text where Stewart and Young craft sentences or paragraphs that help their readers understand the information.
  - Reread page 14. The writers clearly explain the process of how the cocoa flowers bloom. Each sentence tells about a specific part of the process, which helps readers follow along with the way sunlight and sugar sap provide the tree with energy. The words "That's how" in the final sentence help the reader understand they've reached the end of the process and the detailed explanation.
  - Reread page 18. The text on this page suggests that each sentence is a step in a recipe, which makes it accessible to readers. Ask students, "How did the authors invite you to learn about the way the cocoa stems worked on these pages?" You might ask, "What do Stewart and Young do that makes them sound like knowledgeable teachers on these pages?"
- Invite students to use a teaching tone in their writing by providing clear explanations of how things work. Encourage them to break complex information into steps and to employ transitional phrases to make it easier for the reader to understand what's being explained.

| **Power Craft Move:** | Text Features |

| **Name the craft:** | Graphic Style |

| **Why authors do it:** | When writing an informational book, it's important to think about how to present information to readers. Writers and illustrators can embed more information using graphics. |

| **How to do this:** | • Reread what the bookworms say on a few different pages in *No Monkeys, No Chocolate*. As you go through the examples, point out the following: |

- On page 13, the bookworms reinforce the science concept about the importance of the midges. The bookworms also add humor (e.g., echo).
- On page 21, the bookworms reinforce the idea from page 20. This time the bookworm with the hat is the one cracking a joke.
- On page 25, the bookworm with the hat is making a joke again, whereas the one with the tutu reinforces the concept about the fungi.
- On page 29, the bookworm with the hat connects the monkeys to the title of the book, whereas the one with the tutu recaps the final page of the book and makes sense of the content for readers.

- Invite students who have finished revising and editing to add a graphic in order to add another layer of meaning to their writing. Naturally, students might wish to use bookworms, but you can encourage them to add any other kind of comic-book style elements that will enhance the meaning of the text.

| **Power Craft Move:** | Topics and Subtopics |

| **Name the craft:** | Grouping Related Information into Categories |

| **Why authors do it:** | One way many authors break up their topics is by categorizing related information. Writers divide their knowledge into categories even if they don't use traditional headings. |

| **How to do this:** | • Study the following examples with students. |

- Reread page 8. The text and the illustrations focus on cocoa pods. Ask students, "How does the sentence in larger

> print help you figure out what these pages are mostly about?"
> - Reread page 14. Ask students, "What is this page mostly about?" It may help to ask students to identify the big idea and the supporting details.
>   - Look at page 16 ("... and maggots.") and ask students how they could figure out what this page is about based on the big idea featured on page 14 ("Cocoa flowers can't bloom without cocoa leaves ...").
> - Invite students to divide the knowledge they have about their topic into different categories. As Stewart and Young do, they can use introductory sentences (pages 8 and 14) to help readers understand what the information in a given section will be about.

See What a Seal Can Do by Chris Butterworth and Kate Nelms

Publisher's Summary: On the shore, a seal looks like a slow, dozy creature that spends its time lazing around or flumping along the sand. But underwater, it's a different story. Splash! Seal dives deep, with a body just the right shape to shoot through the water and power down with his back flippers. He slips through a seaweed forest, and—sensing a predator nearby—dives even deeper to stay safe. Finally it's time to make a sudden twist and turn to catch his fishy dinner. Merging a lyrical narrative sprinkled with fascinating facts and awe-inspiring illustrations, here is one nature adventure that's hard to resist. Back matter includes an index.

Power Craft Move: Back Matter

Name the craft: Author's Note

Why authors do it: Some authors write narrative nonfiction, which are stories about animals or real-life events. Sometimes the stories follow the exact sequence of events and sometimes they're embellished. Writers can include an author's note along with their text to help readers glean all the facts about the topic.

How to do this:
- Reread the author's note on page 4. Invite students to think about what kinds of things they learned about wild seals from this note.

- At the conclusion of rereading, point out the following:
  - Seals are mammals that live partly on land and partly in water.
  - There are physical differences between fur seals, sea lions, and true seals.
  - There are eighteen kinds of true seals, all of which are pictured at the end of the book.
  - This book is about gray seals, which once were hunted but are now protected by many countries.
- The note about wild seals is Butterworth's way of sharing more information about seals with readers. Because the captions are about the illustrations in the text and there are no other text features, additional facts about wild seals are best included in the back matter.
- Help students figure out what is important for the main body of work versus what should be left for the author's note.
- Invite students to look through their note cards to determine what they want to tell in the main piece of their writing and what are interesting facts that might not fit with the majority of their information. Students can create two piles: *fits with the majority of the writing I'm doing* and *fits better in an author's note*. From there, students can write some of the facts about their subject for inclusion in an author's note.

Power Craft Move:	Content-Specific Vocabulary
Name the craft:	Technical Language Teaches Readers About Topics
Why authors do it:	Nonfiction writers use technical language to teach their readers more about a topic. The technical language must be defined for a reader.
How to do this:	• Study at least two places in *See What a Seal Can Do* where Butterworth embeds technical language and includes the definitions of those terms.

  - On page 6, the word *flumping* is used. On page 7, Butterworth defines the word *flump* in parentheses. Ask students if they understand what flumping looks like based on the definition on page 7.
  - Reread the caption about mammals on page 7. Adding the words *like us* after the comma helps readers understand that seals are like people. Butterworth adds another sentence that

explains that seals are warm-blooded and breathe air, both characteristics of mammals.

- Reread the caption on page 16. The definition of *molt* occurs in the middle of the sentence. Commas separate the definition from the rest of the information.

- Invite students to embed definitions for technical language they want to include in their texts, as Butterworth does. They can use commas to offset the definition or add another sentence to define the terminology.

Power Craft Move:	Ending
Name the craft:	Circular Ending and The Way We Are Known Ending
Why authors do it:	Writers often combine two types of endings in their writing. A circular ending brings the writing back to where it began. In addition, writers often end their writing by focusing on the major accomplishments, qualities, or attributes of the subject.
How to do this:	• Reread pages 26–28 to your students. Show students the similarities between these lines and those from the lead (pages 6 and 8). The word *so* is Butterworth's way of wrapping up everything she's told us about seals. The final sentence includes similes that compare seals to two unlike things.
	• The final line recaps what we learned about seals in the book. It's a "way we are known" ending because it helps readers to make a discovery about the seal. For example, he might look like sluggish sunbather, but he's not.
	• Invite students to try writing a circular or "way we are known" ending, using *See What a Seal Can Do* as a mentor text. Encourage them to consider repeating part of the lead using figurative language to recap everything their readers have learned about the subject.
Power Craft Move:	Lead
Name the craft:	Meeting the Characters
Why authors do it:	In nonfiction as well as fiction writing, authors bring readers into the world of the story by introducing the main characters immediately.

How to do this:
- Reread pages 6–8 with students. We get a strong sense of what the seal does on land. There's a simile that compares the seal to a fat sunbather, but readers quickly learn that seals are not lazy animals. On page 8, readers learn seals spend most of their time in the sea looking for food, which is hard work. On pages 6–8 readers meet the main character, Seal, and then go on an adventure with him.
- Invite your small group to draft a meeting-the-characters lead. Encourage students to put the main character in a setting, doing something typical. Encourage them to give readers just enough information to interact with the main character throughout the rest of their writing.

Power Craft Move: Precise Words

Name the craft: Vivid Verbs

Why authors do it: Vivid verbs show readers precisely what is happening in a piece of writing.

How to do this:
- Study at least two of the following places in the text:
  - On page 11, "His back flippers *power* him one hundred feet down in seconds." The word *power* conveys the seal's strength.
  - On page 12, "Seal *slips* through the seaweed forest—big eyes searching the gloom." The word *slips* helps readers picture the seal moving effortlessly through the seaweed, which is too dense for other creatures to get through.
  - On page 19, "He *swallows* a few sand eels and waits to see what else might turn up." The word *swallows* helps us envision the seal gulping down the eels without chewing first.
  - Debrief with students. Talk about how specific words produce better writing than vague ones.
- Invite students to replace vague verbs with stronger ones in their writing. Encourage them to choose verbs to help their readers envision the actions happening. In addition, remind students to use stronger and more precise verbs going forward.

Power Craft Move: Punctuation to Create Voice

Name the craft: Em Dashes

Why authors do it: Writers use dashes to emphasize, interrupt, or change a thought in the middle of a sentence. An em dash dramatically introduces extra material to a sentence.

How to do this:
- Study at least two of the following places in the text:
  - On page 10, "When you dive, you have to take a big breath in—but a seal blows its breath out." A dash adds surprising information to the sentence.
  - On page 12, "Seal slips through the seaweed forest—big eyes searching the gloom." Hypothesize that the author uses the phrase after the dash to emphasize the seal's senses. The text provides a vivid image for readers.
  - On page 21, "Up he swims, whiskers twitching, ears sharp, eyes wide—and spies some stragglers on the edge of a mackerel shoal." The presence of the dash, along with the previous bits of text and the illustration, suggests that something big is going to happen.
  - On page 28, "Seal can dive like a rocket and twist like a dancer—he's a super-swimming underwater wonder!" The text after the dash emphasizes the seal's grandeur.
- Invite students to insert em dashes into their writing where they want to emphasize something, change their thought, interrupt themselves, or add something dramatic to the text.

Power Craft Move: Punctuation to Create Voice

Name the craft: Ellipses Points

Why authors do it: Writers use ellipsis points when they want a sentence to trail off.

How to do this:
- Study both places in the text where the author used ellipsis points in this way:
  - Reread the main text on page 9. Butterworth may have wanted to lead readers into the next page slowly. Ask students why she might want them to linger. Point out how the ellipsis points on this page follow the period.
  - Reread the main text on page 25. Hypothesize that Butterworth is trying to get readers to slow down, just as the seal has slowed down in the book. Talk about the way ellipses affect a reader's pacing.

- Note: The ellipsis points on page 19 are used differently.
- Invite students to examine their writing. Encourage them to use ellipses as a way to get readers to adjust their pacing before leading them to the next sentence.

Power Craft Move:	Repetition

Name the craft: Repeated Phrase

Why authors do it: Writers repeat language or an idea when they want to emphasize something for the reader. Sometimes writers repeat a word, a phrase, or a few sentences throughout the text.

How to do this:
- Study both places where Butterworth repeats a phrase. (Note: Butterworth uses the word *but* several times throughout the text. The following examples repeat a phrase that begins with *but*.)
  - On pages 8 and 26–28 we read: "And you might think a seal's just a slow, dozy creature that spends its time lazing around. But you'd be wrong!"
    - Hypothesize about the reasons this line is repeated at the end of the book. Perhaps it was to contradict the stereotypes or misinformation people have about seals. Or maybe Butterworth does it as a way to catch the reader's attention. Another idea could be that Butterworth wants to make the final sentence stand out for the reader.
- Invite students to choose a phrase in two or more places in their writing. Some students might be tempted to talk directly to the reader with a "But you'd be wrong!" type of sentence. If that works for the student's writing, that's fine, but encourage students to create phrases to emphasize something important for their readers rather than merely copying Butterworth's exact language.

Power Craft Move:	Text Features

Name the craft: Fact Inserts

Why authors do it: Writers insert facts to explain an illustration or to give the reader additional information.

How to do this: • There are fact inserts on nearly every page of the text. Two examples:
- Examine page 9 with your small group. Read aloud the fact in the bottom right corner of the page. The information references the illustration. The seal is flumping down the beach, by himself, toward the water.
- Reread the fact inserts on page 22. *Both* of the facts on this page provide a greater explanation for what's happening in the illustration. This enhances our understanding of how seals eat.
- Invite students to insert facts to enhance the meaning of the illustrations they create for readers.

The Slug by Elise Gravel

Publisher's Summary: One in a series of humorous books about disgusting creatures, *The Slug* is a look at the land slug. It covers such topics as the slug's two pairs of tentacles, one pair for seeing, one pair for smelling (it can see you're a kid and smell things, like broccoli), its breathing hole (on the side of its head!), and its pretty gross mucous covering (in order to find a partner, the slug can follow another slug's mucous trail. True love!). Although silly and off-the-wall, *The Slug* contains real information that will tie in with curriculum.

Power Craft Move: Content-Specific Vocabulary

Name the craft: Technical Language Teaches Readers About Topics

Why authors do it: Nonfiction writers infuse their writing with technical language to teach their readers more about topics. A writer usually defines technical language for readers.

How to do this: • Study two places in *The Slug* where Gravel embeds technical language.
- Reread page 12. Show readers how Gravel defines *retractable* on the page. Point out the pattern: a comma, followed by "which means," and then a definition. Note that it is a kid-friendly definition rather than a dictionary one. Point out the picture, which shows how the slug retracts its tentacles, enhancing the definition of the word.

- Reread page 18. A technical definition for *mucus* follows in the text. Point out how the parenthetical reference, "kind of like snot," provides a slang word that most children understand. Show students how the comma after *mucus* gets readers ready for the definition.
- Invite students to embed definitions for technical language in their texts, as Gravel does. They can use a comma to help readers know when they're going to encounter a new word. They can also use phrases such as "which means" to help readers know that a technical term is being defined.

Power Craft Move: Ending

Name the craft: Advice to the Reader

Why authors do it: Nonfiction writers may offer advice or words of wisdom to their readers at the end of their texts. This type of ending offers readers a chance to reconsider how they thought about something or to see it in a different way.

How to do this:
- Reread pages 30–31. Make note of Gravel telling readers to be kind to slugs on page 30. Perhaps the ending is this way to encourage readers to consider the important role slugs play in the environment.
- Invite students to offer words of wisdom to their readers by writing an ending that serves as advice to readers. Encourage them to think about their audience and offer advice without sounding preachy or combative. Have students try out this kind of ending while they're gathered with you and encourage them to share what they've written with the group to make sure their words of wisdom are firm without being didactic.

Power Craft Move: Lead

Name the craft: Talking to the Reader

Why authors do it: Nonfiction writers can talk directly to their audience to get their attention. Doing this helps them connect with their readers and introduce the content.

How to do this: • Study pages 4 and 5 with students. Discuss Gravel's addressing readers as "Ladies and gentlemen." Point out how the narrator's voice uses the first-person word *me*. Make a note that slugs are the focus the book. This gets readers ready to interact with the big idea of the text. Show readers the slug addressing readers both by looking at them and through the use of a speech bubble.
  • Invite your small group to try a talking to the reader lead. Encourage students to address their audience by writing in the first person. Students can also try tweaking a general address, such as "ladies and gentlemen," in their writing. Remind students to introduce the topic to readers in the lead of their writing as well.

Power Craft Move: Precise Words

Name the craft: Vivid Verbs

Why authors do it: Vivid verbs show readers precisely what is happening in a piece of writing.

How to do this: • Study at least two of the following places in the text:
  • On pages 4 and 5, "Ladies and gentlemen, let me *introduce* the slug." *Introduce* helps the author present the topic of the book, getting readers get ready to learn more about land slugs.
  • On page 16, "The slug *moves* by contracting the muscles in its belly." The word *moves* and the rest of the information on the page help readers comprehend how the slug propels itself forward.
    • Because the book is for young readers, the word *moves* is more appropriate than *propels*. Talk to students about a strong verb also being one readers can comprehend.
  • On page 22, "The slug *produces* extra mucus so it becomes more slippery . . . ." The word *produces* helps readers understand that the mucus enables the slug to escape from the predator's grasp.
  • Debrief with students. Talk about the specificity of words such as *introduce, move,* and *produces*. Help students think about these precise verbs in contrast to vague verbs.

- If you didn't use the example from page 16, note that verbs don't have to be big and fancy to be strong and specific. (This will help students resist the temptation to turn to a thesaurus, which doesn't guarantee stronger writing.)
- Invite students to replace vague verbs with stronger ones in their writing. Encourage them to choose verbs that will help their readers envision the action. In addition, remind students to work toward drafting with stronger and more precise verbs going forward.

Power Craft Move:	Teaching Tone

Name the craft: Clear Explanations

Why authors do it: Writers connect with readers by using a consistent tone in their writing. One way writers do this is by providing clear explanations of how things work so their readers can learn from their writing.

How to do this:
- Study two places where Gravel crafts page spreads to help readers understand the information being provided.
    - Examine pages 22 and 23 with students. The illustration shows a slug squirting extra mucus, which will help readers understand a slug's defense mechanism. The expression on the slug's face gives readers a sense of the danger it's escaping, which enhances the text on page 22. Combining a relevant illustration, speech bubble, and text gives readers a better understanding of how slugs protect themselves from predators.
    - Reread pages 28 and 29. Gravel explains that farmers and gardeners dislike slugs because they eat their lettuce. Next, Gravel explains that slugs break down decaying plants, which turns them back into nutrients for the soil. This example gives readers a concrete way to understand the magical role that slugs play in helping the environment. (Hence the magician's hat, wand, and related speech bubble on page 29.) Using a concrete example is one way writers help readers understand a complex idea.
- Invite students to use a teaching tone in their writing by providing a clear explanation of how things work for their readers. Encourage students to explain complex information in a way that combines words, other text features, and even humor. Have students pick a place in their writing where they can do a better job

of teaching their reader about something. They may continue this work at their seats. Once they finish, encourage them to read their explanation to someone unfamiliar with their text (not their writing partners) and then ask them if they understand the information.

Power Craft Move: Text Features

Name the craft: Print Layout

Why authors do it: When writing an informational book, it's important to think about how to present information to readers.

How to do this:
- Examine some page spreads from *The Slug* where Gravel communicates facts on the lefthand page and funny, storylike addresses from the slug on the righthand one. (The exceptions to this rule are on pages 8–9, 10–11, 20–21, and 24–25.) Two places you can study with students:
    - On pages 6 and 7, point out how the illustration and speech bubble on page 7 help readers understand the meaning of the word *mollusk,* which is undefined, on page 6. Although the snail is saying something funny to the mollusk, he's also helping readers understand that mollusks are animals with a soft body and no backbone.
    - On pages 26 and 27, readers learn slugs are both male and female. The illustration of the slug is a play on what nurses and doctors tell a new mom after she gives birth. There, in the hospital bed, the nurse tells the slug patient that the baby slug is a "boy-girl." This funny illustration reinforces the idea of the slug's being both male and female.
- Invite students to decide how to structure the pages in their informational books. Encourage them to use illustrations and speech bubbles, as Gravel does, to enhance the meaning of the words for their readers.
    - Remind students that this kind of layout should function as a teaching tool for readers, not just provide laughs.

Power Craft Move: Topics and Subtopics

Name the craft: Grouping Related Information and Illustrations

Why authors do it: Nonfiction writers teach readers about a big topic. Writers and illustrators create categories by grouping related information and illustrations when they're writing an informational book.

How to do this:
- Study two places in *The Slug* where Gravel grouped related information and illustrations.
  - Pages 10–13 are all about the slug's tentacles. Although the header doesn't say "tentacles," the word is written in large letters across the top of page 10. Tentacles are defined and explained on page 10 and pictured on page 11. On pages 12–13, readers learn about retractable tentacles.
  - Pages 18–25 focus on mucus. Again, the header doesn't say "mucus," but the word is written in large letters on page 18. The next few page spreads are about mucus. On pages 18–19, Gravel defines mucus. On pages 20–21, she explains how mucus helps slugs move. On pages 22–23, readers learn how mucus protects slugs from predators. On pages 24–25, readers learn how mucus helps slugs reproduce.
    - It might help to use boxes and bullets to help readers see that mucus is the big topic, and the rest are the subtopics. For instance:

Mucus

      - Movement
      - Protection
      - Reproduction
- Invite students to narrow the information they've collected and divide it into different topics or subtopics or categories. Encourage them to group related information and drawings under these categories.

Afterword:
An Invitation
to Collaborate

This book was a long time in the making. It started with a conversation in August 2012 and grew from there. I did my best during that time to read hundreds of picture books so I could find the best possible teaching companions for use in elementary writing workshops. Although I believe the choices are strong, new books may emerge to serve as mentor texts. I will continue to review mentor texts on my blog, Two Writing Teachers, but I also welcome your ideas.

Let's collaborate in the years to come. Please let me know about your discoveries by reaching out to me on Twitter, @sshubitz (use #craftmoves in your Tweet). I hope we can join forces with other teachers and coaches who've read this book to uncover the best ways to use new picture books with kids during writing workshop.

Glossary

Author's Note: Additional information created by the author to accompany a text. An author's note is usually found at the back of a book. Author's notes provide readers with additional information or an insider's perspective about the text.

Back Matter: Text that comes after the last page of the story or main text. Examples of back matter include the author/illustrator note, fact pages, historical notes, and source lists.

Beginning-Middle-End: Stories have distinct parts. Characters and the setting are usually introduced at the beginning of stories. Readers find out what happens to the characters in the middle. By the end of stories, characters usually change in some way.

Cadence: A way writers stress or emphasize points in their writing. The rhythm of writing pushes readers forward, which keeps them engaged.

Call-to-Action Page: Authors anticipate their writing will make readers care about an issue. A call-to-action page is a list of suggestions to help readers take action once they finish reading.

Captions: The text beneath a picture or photograph that enhances the reader's understanding of the image.

Categories: Chunks of related information that help readers understand a larger topic; subdivisions of a topic.

Character Details: Information about what characters are doing, thinking, or feeling.

Citations: Responsible writers document material that isn't their own by letting readers know the original source of their quoted or paraphrased material.

Clear Explanations: A concise, easy-to-understand way of explaining information to readers.

Code Switching: The practice of alternating between two languages in writing.

Colon, then commas in a list: Colons can introduce lists after writers have written a complete sentence. The information that precedes the colon must be able to stand alone.

Commas: Commas help readers figure out which words go together in a sentence, which parts of a sentence are most important, and which parts can be used in lists, to add details, or to state when or where something happens.

Content-Specific Words: Technical language that helps readers to understand the topic. Often, content-specific words are defined in context, in a sidebar, or in a book's glossary.

Dashes: Horizontal lines used to emphasize, interrupt, or change a thought in the middle of a sentence. Dashes can be used to set off part of the text so as to draw attention to it. Dashes are also used to create longer or more dramatic pauses before a page turn. It's important to ensure that sentences will make sense if the words between the dashes are removed from the sentence. Dashes can also substitute for parentheses.

Defining Words in Context: Technical language defined in the writing. Definitions can be offset with commas, dashes, or parentheses.

Dialogue: The spoken words between characters in a story. Dialogue is an elaboration tool that helps writers to move the story forward because readers can hear the exchange of language between characters.

Ellipsis Points: Three spaced points, or dots, which indicate a pause or suspension of thought. The markings slow readers down, make the voice trail off, or cause the reader to read with different expression. Ellipsis points can also indicate the omission of a word, phrase, line, and so on.

Em Dashes: Longer dashes used to emphasize, interrupt, or change a thought in the middle of a sentence. An em dash dramatically introduces extra material to a sentence.

Endings: The final line, lines, or pages of a book that conclude a piece and stay with readers. Some examples of types of endings:

- Accomplishments/Discovery: An ending that shows how the main character has changed for the better by the end of the story.
- Advice to the Reader: Words of wisdom or advice offered to readers at the end of writing. This type of ending offers

readers a chance to reconsider how they thought about something or to see it in a different way.

- Circular: The action of the story returns to themes shared at the beginning. Essentially, the writing ends where it began.
- Connecting with the Reader: An upbeat way to end a book by connecting to readers in a personal way.
- Final Action: An ending that shows the character(s) engaged in one final action.
- Lesson Learned: The conclusion shows a character who has changed or grown from an experience.
- Summary List: A recap of the main ideas to remind readers of all the things they learned from a text.
- Surprise: An ending readers do not see coming.
- The Way We Are Known: The conclusion focuses on the major accomplishments, qualities, or attributes of the person, object, or animal featured in the writing.
- Wondering: A wrap-up of a story that provides space for readers to ponder what will happen in the future.
- Wraparound: An ending that provides an echo or a whisper of the lead on the final pages of the book. This kind of ending acts as a bookend to the lead.

Fact Inserts: Facts that provide an explanation for an illustration or give the reader additional information.

Fact Page: An additional page—usually in the back of a text—where writers can share additional information to deepen readers' understanding of the text.

Graphic Style: A style that allows writers and illustrators to embed another layer of information into a text using a design element.

Grouping Related Information and Illustrations: Writing and illustrations chunked together to teach readers about an aspect of a big topic.

Heading: The name of a category that tells readers what a section of writing (and illustrations) will be about.

Heart of the Story: The most important part of a narrative, which is often revealed bit by bit rather than through a summary.

Historical Note: A way to provide readers with additional information about a time period or the backstory to someone's life.

Hyphenated Words: Two or more words joined together to form a compound adjective that is often more descriptive and distinctive than an ordinary, one-word modifier.

Information Page: An additional page of text, usually at the end of a book, where readers can learn more about a topic.

Internal Thinking: The inner thoughts of a character, which are often reflected in self-dialogue.

Inside Dashes: An em dash or pair of em dashes used to offset additional information provided to readers within a text. Inside dashes can be used instead of commas.

Leads: The first line, lines, or pages of a book that hook readers and make them want to read on. Some examples of leads:

- Action: A form of movement to invite readers into the world of the story.
- Appeal to the Senses: Helping readers feel as if they're hearing, touching, seeing, smelling, or tasting something from the moment they begin reading.
- Asking a Question: Engaging readers with a question in the beginning of the writing.
- Character Snapshot: Bringing readers into the world of the story by revealing information about the main character(s).
- Compare/Contrast: A way to draw readers into a story by comparing and contrasting two things to get a sense of the world.
- Definition: Terminology that builds readers' schemas and enables them to interact with the text that follows.
- Developing Setting/Creating a Sense of Era: A way to help readers understand where a narrative takes place by layering the lead with dates or events.
- Imagine: A way to transport readers to other places by encouraging them to imagine something out of the ordinary.
- Letter to the Reader: An introduction that gets readers ready to interact with material. This kind of lead makes readers feel as if the author is speaking directly to them to make the purpose for writing the book clear.
- Meeting the Characters: An immediate introduction to the main or secondary characters.
- Setting Details: A vivid description of where or when the story takes place.
- Sharing a Secret: A lead that tells readers something to make them feel privy to the inside world of the story.
- Simile: A rich description that compares two unlike things using *like* or *as*.

- Taking a Reader into the Past: Transporting readers to a long-ago time.
- Talking to the Reader: A way to gain readers' attention by talking directly to them.

Maps and Pictures: Text features to deepen readers' understanding and interaction with a nonfiction text.

Movement of Time and Place: A technique that transitions readers from place to place and through time in a story that has multiple scenes and settings.

Pacing: Controlling the speed at which one tells a story. Some parts are written purposefully slow, whereas other parts are written in a way to make readers move faster.

Parentheses: Authors add these markings to clarify something for readers. They're also a way of making the writer's voice more conversational.

Partial Quotes: A way to cite part of the real words a character says. Quotation marks are used to differentiate what is spoken from the rest of the text.

Power of Three: The repetition of a word, phrase, or action three times to draw attention to something in the text. Many people believe that three repetitions of something in writing make the writing funnier, more memorable, or more satisfying to readers.

Precise Information: Specific information about what characters are doing in order to make the writing come alive for readers.

Precise Words: Specific words used to add power to writing.

Print Layout: The way text and illustrations are presented on the page.

Punctuation to Create Voice: Writers create a mood in their writing by making conscious decisions about the kind of punctuation to use. When writers make purposeful choices about their punctuation, their writing sounds the way they intend.

Quotation Sources: A reference list, usually included in the back matter, to help readers with the correct attribution of quotes.

Quotes and Sources: Responsible writers keep track of the quotes they use and material they cite from other texts. Writers document this information in a bibliography or works cited list, which usually comes at the end of their published writing.

Refrain: Lines that repeat throughout texts to showcase a particularly strong idea. Repeating a line, or a refrain, at several points can help readers come away with the big idea or message.

Repetition: A recurring word, phrase, or line that has a desired effect.

Rule of Three: A way to create a rhythmic quality to writing by using sets of three: three actions, a sequence of three things, three characters, and so on. Anything done three distinct times tends to draw a reader's attention to a section of text.

Semicolon: A punctuation mark that separates closely related clauses. Semicolons add variety to writing and can replace successive choppy sentences that end with periods.

Sensory Details: Writing that appeals to the five senses by creating concrete images so the writing comes to life.

Setting Details: Writing that provides readers with a sense of place through vivid descriptions of settings, including the period, weather, location, or time of day.

Specific Details: Carefully chosen words that help readers envision what is being described or explained.

Show, Don't Tell: Instead of stating what's happening, an author uses action, internal thinking, dialogue, and figurative language to help readers envision what's happening in the text.

Specific Nouns: Precise words that help readers understand exact people, places, or things.

Speech Balloons: Writing that can be infused with technical language to teach readers more about a topic. Speech balloons are a text feature that can be used to embed the definitions for technical language on a separate part of the page.

Speech Bubbles: A way to allow characters' voices to be heard in a story while moving the plotline forward. Quotation marks and dialogue tags are not used with speech bubbles because they stem from the illustration of the person talking.

Structure: The way the parts of a piece work together. Structural examples include: thinking about the way the beginning-middle-end of a story is weighted, sequencing the story, stretching out the heart of a story, and moving a reader through time and place. Well-structured writing enhances a piece's meaning.

Talking to the Audience: Phrases directed to readers; used to explain the author's thinking and engage with the reader.

Teaching Tone: An engaging, consistent tone used throughout a piece of writing, which teaches a reader without undermining their prior knowledge about a topic.

Technical Language: Content-specific words defined in context or in a glossary.

Text Features: A way to organize and present information to readers. Text features can include a table of contents, headings, labels, time lines, captions, different types of print, glossaries, and so on.

Time Lines: A text feature that shows past events in chronological order. Time lines help readers understand when specific events happened during a given time period.

Topics and Subtopics: Writers make choices about what they're going to teach their audience. Often, writers will divide their big idea into smaller sections, which helps readers digest the different aspects of their big idea.

Turning Point (or Pivot Point): Turning (or pivot) points are those defining moments when something of great significance happens to the main character or when she or he has an epiphany. A turning point often moves the story forward in that this is often a time when the main character changes in a significant way.

Types of Print: The variation of print (e.g., color, size, italics) in a text. Print is varied in order to create a desired effect for readers.

Varied Sentence Lengths: Writing is more lyrical, dramatic, and fun to read when sentences do not all conform to size. Writers vary the length of their sentences in order to communicate meaning and tone to their readers and because it can make writing more interesting to read.

Vivid Verbs: Precise words that show the actions happening in a piece of writing. Selecting the strongest verb possible can add power to a sentence.

Vocative Case: A direct address to a person or a thing that can occur in the beginning, middle, or end of a sentence. Writers use commas to offset the name of the person or thing being addressed in a sentence.

Bibliography

Picture Books

Adderson, Caroline. 2015. *Eat, Leo! Eat!* Illus. Josée Bisaillon. Toronto: Kids Can Press.

Aston, Dianna H. 2012. *A Rock Is Lively*. Illus. Sylvia Long. San Francisco: Chronicle Books.

Boelts, Maribeth. 2012. *Happy Like Soccer*. Illus. Lauren Castillo. Somerville, MA: Candlewick.

Bradley, Sandra. 2015. *Henry Holton Takes the Ice*. Illus. Sara Palacios. New York: Dial.

Bryant, Jen. 2013. *A Splash of Red: The Life and Art of Horace Pippin*. Illus. Melissa Sweet. New York: Alfred A. Knopf.

Bunting, Eve. 2015. *Yard Sale*. Illus. Lauren Castillo. Somerville, MA: Candlewick.

Butterworth, Chris. 2013. *See What a Seal Can Do*. Illus. Kate Nelms. Somerville, MA: Candlewick.

Cox, Lynne. 2014. *Elizabeth, Queen of the Seas*. Illus. Brian Floca. New York: Schwartz & Wade.

de la Peña, Matt. 2015. *Last Stop on Market Street*. Illus. Christian Robinson. New York: G. P. Putnam's Sons.

Fleming, Candace. 2010. *Clever Jack Takes the Cake*. Illus. G. Brian Karas. New York: Schwartz & Wade.

Goldstone, Bruce. 2015. *I See A Pattern Here*. New York: Henry Holt.

Gravel, Elise. 2014. *The Slug*. Toronto: Tundra Books.

Kearney, Meg. 2013. *Trouper*. Illus. E. B. Lewis. New York: Scholastic Press.

Medina, Meg. 2015. *Mango, Abuela, and Me*. Illus. Angela
   Dominguez. Somerville, MA: Candlewick.
Roberts, Cokie. 2014. *Founding Mothers: Remembering the Ladies*.
   Illus. Diane Goode. New York: Harper.
Saxby, Claire. 2015. *Big Red Kangaroo*. Somerville, MA: Candlewick.
Schiffer, Miriam B. 2015. *Stella Brings the Family*. Illus. Holly
   Clifton-Brown. San Francisco: Chronicle Books.
Simon, Seymour. 2013. *Coral Reefs*. New York: Harper.
Stewart, Melissa, and Allen Young. 2013. *No Monkeys, No
   Chocolate*. Illus. Nicole Wong. Watertown, MA: Charlesbridge.
Willems, Mo. 2010. *Knuffle Bunny Free: An Unexpected Diversion*.
   New York: Balzer & Bray.

Professional References

Anderson, Carl. 2000. *How's It Going? A Practical Guide to
   Conferring with Student Writers*. Portsmouth, NH: Heinemann.
———. 2005. *Assessing Writers*. Portsmouth, NH: Heinemann.
Ayres, Ruth, and Stacey Shubitz. 2010. *Day by Day: Refining Writing
   Workshop Through 180 Days of Reflective Practice*. Portland,
   ME: Stenhouse.
Bishop, R. S. 1990. "Mirrors, Windows, and Sliding Glass Doors."
   Perspectives: Choosing and Using Books for the Classroom 6 (3):
   ix–xi.
Bomer, Katherine. 2010. *Hidden Gems: Naming and Teaching from
   the Brilliance in Every Student's Writing*. Portsmouth, NH:
   Heinemann.
Buckner, Aimee D. 1999. "Using Authors as Mentors." *Primary
   Voices* 7 (4): 7–10.
Caine, Karen. 2008. *Writing to Persuade: Minilessons to Help
   Students Plan, Draft, and Revise, Grades 3–8*. Portsmouth, NH:
   Heinemann.
Calkins, Lucy. 1994. *The Art of Teaching Writing, New Edition*.
   Portsmouth, NH: Heinemann.
———. 2013. A *Guide to the Common Core Writing Workshop:
   Intermediate Grades*. Portsmouth, NH: Heinemann.
Calkins, Lucy McCormick. 2001. *The Art of Teaching Reading*. New
   York: Addison-Wesley.
Cruz, M. Colleen. 2015. *The Unstoppable Writing Teacher: Real
   Strategies for the Real Classroom*. Portsmouth, NH: Heinemann.

Dorfman, Lynne. 2015. Telephone interview, April 17.

Dorfman, Lynne R., and Rose Cappelli. 2007. *Mentor Texts: Teaching Writing Through Children's Literature, K–6.* Portland, ME: Stenhouse.

———. 2009. *Nonfiction Mentor Texts: Teaching Informational Writing Through Children's Literature, K–8.* Portland, ME: Stenhouse.

Eickholdt, Lisa. 2015. *Learning from Classmates: Using Students' Writing as Mentor Texts.* Portsmouth, NH: Heinemann.

Feigelson, Dan. 2008. *Practical Punctuation: Lessons on Rule Making and Rule Breaking in Elementary Writing.* Portsmouth, NH: Heinemann.

Fletcher, Ralph. 2011. *Mentor Author, Mentor Texts: Short Texts, Craft Notes, and Practical Classroom Uses.* Portsmouth, NH: Heinemann.

Heard, Georgia. 2014. *The Revision Toolbox: Teaching Techniques That Work.* 2nd edition. Portsmouth, NH: Heinemann.

Hubbard, B. 2013. "Building Stamina in Primary Writers." December 20. https://twowritingteachers.wordpress.com/2013/12/20/buildingstamina/.

Laminack, Lester L., and Reba M. Wadsworth. 2006. *Reading Aloud Across the Curriculum: How to Build Bridges in Language Arts, Math, Science, and Social Studies.* Portsmouth, NH: Heinemann.

Messner, Kate. 2009. "Authors Who Skype with Classes & Book Clubs (for Free!)." May 28. http://www.katemessner.com/authors-who-skype-with-classes-book-clubs-for-free/.

Murphy, Dana. 2014. "Don't Skip Share Time." August 9. https://twowritingteachers.wordpress.com/2014/08/09/sharpen-your-workshop-routines-dont-skip-share-time/.

National Governors Association Center for Best Practices (NGA) and Council of Chief State School Officers (CCSSO). 2010. *Common Core State Standards for English Language Arts and Literacy in History/Social Studies, Science, and Technical Subjects: Appendix A: Research Supporting Key Elements of the Standards; Glossary of Key Terms.* Washington, DC: NGA and CCSSO.

Ray, Katie Wood. 1999. *Wondrous Words: Writers and Writing in the Elementary Classroom.* Urbana, IL: NCTE.

———. 2006. *Study Driven: A Framework for Planning Units of Study in the Writing Workshop.* Portsmouth, NH: Heinemann.

————. (2008. "Teaching Tip: Katie Wood Ray on Building Writers' Stamina." August 25. Retrieved from https://youtu.be/y4KIcbOe5kQ.

Shubitz, Stacey. 2008. "Meta-Language for Talking About Texts." August 12. https://twowritingteachers.wordpress.com/2008/08/12/meta-language-for-talking-about-texts/.

————. 2012. "Writing Workshop Expectations." August 23. https://twowritingteachers.wordpress.com/2012/08/23/wwexpectations/.

————. 2015. "The Cupcake Metaphor." August 16. https://twowritingteachers.wordpress.com/2015/08/16/the-cupcake-metaphor/.

We Need Diverse Books. 2015. Mission Statement. http://weneeddiversebooks.org/mission-statement/.

Wilson, Margaret Berry. 2012. *Interactive Modeling: A Powerful Technique for Teaching Children*. Turners Falls, MA: Center for Responsive Schools, Inc.

Credits

Index

Page numbers followed by *f* indicate figures.